Three Centuries of Change

BRITISH SOCIAL AND ECONOMIC HISTORY SINCE 1700

RICH   NDY MOORE

Collins Educational

An imprint of HarperCollins*Publishers*

Published by Collins Educational
An imprint of HarperCollins Publishers Ltd
77-85 Fulham Palace Road
Hammersmith
London W6 8JB

© HarperCollins Publishers Ltd 1998

First published 1998

ISBN 000327113 7

Richard Staton, Ray Ennion and Wendy Moore assert the moral right to be identified as the authors of this work.

British Library Cataloguing in Publication Data
A catalogue record for this publication is available from the British Library.

Edited by Joanne Stone
Design by Sally Boothroyd
Cover design by Derek Lee
Map artwork and original illustrations by Raymond Turvey
Graphs by Barking Dog Art
Picture research by Caroline Thompson
Production by Sue Cashin
Printed by Printing Express Ltd, Hong Kong.

CONTENTS

INTRODUCTION

This book leads you through the main changes which transformed Britain during the last three centuries.

Britain in 1700

Britain was mainly a country of villages. Most people were poor farmers who owned small strips of land and scratched a living from the soil. They lived in draughty, damp and overcrowded cottages, which had neither a clean water supply nor drains. There were few towns, few industries – apart from the making of tools and woollen cloth – and people rarely travelled very far during their lives. Transport over muddy roads, or on short stretches of river, was difficult, dangerous and uncomfortable. Many men had few legal rights (women had even fewer). Most men could not vote (no women could vote). Very few people could read or write. Death rates were high, and most women, men and children, could only look forward to unhealthy, short lives in damp and dirty conditions.

Britain was a non-industrial country.

The Industrial Revolution

From between the 1740s and the 1780s, things began to change. There was a feeling that this was an exciting time in which to live. The pace of life was quickening. By the time a German called Georg May visited Britain in 1815, he found that there were so many 'interesting things to be seen. There is something new to catch the eye in every step that one takes'. There were powerful machines, factories, coal pits, iron works and – by the 1820s – railways.

Nothing sums up the transformation of Britain better than the **Great Exhibition** in 1851. Over 6 million people visited the Crystal Palace to see it (see Source 2). They marvelled at the best of British invention and technology. The proud display of machines, cloth, furniture, pottery, silverware and steam engines was evidence of British self-confidence – and of British superiority, because many of these things were exported around the world.

However, there was a human price to be paid for this transformation. Britain was becoming a nation of town dwellers, and industrial workers, at an astonishing speed. In 1800 only 25% of the population lived in towns and cities. By the end of the 19th century, that figure was 75%. Workers were drawn away from their familiar villages into towns and sea ports full of people. The old ways of life were disappearing. Tied to the exhausting pace of steam engines, workers finished their shifts only to return to overcrowded rooms or cellars, in housing hastily built with little thought for the health or quality of life of the people living there.

This book is the story of these people and their struggle for better public health, education, trade unions and rights. For women in particular, there were many changes ahead in their role and status in society. For all people, 20th century developments in medicine have, perhaps, made the most striking change in their well being from the people of 1700.

SOURCE 1
Spinning on the village green.

SOURCE 2
The Crystal Palace in Hyde Park, London, which housed the Great Exhibition of 1851. It had 294,000 panes of manufactured glass.

> **Aiming for a higher grade**
> To make progress in GCSE History depends on the understanding of the following points. Think about these as you work through this book.

1 Cause and consequence

Think about: Why something happened. What were the most important reasons for it happening? What were the results? Were they intended to be the results?

● Try to link different reasons (and contributory factors) together.
● Understand why there are different types of causes e.g. political, economic and social.
● Explain why some factors are more important than others.

2 Change over time

Think about: How did things change? What were the factors which led to, or resulted from, the changes?

● Explain how each factor played a part, and explain why, perhaps, one factor is more important and the others are less important.
● Show how all the factors are interlinked.
● Say if things changed quickly or slowly.

3 How to use a source – is it reliable and accurate?

When you look at a source, try to bear in mind, not only what the source tells you, but also why the author or artist wanted to say these things. A source can create all kinds of impressions. Is it trying to influence your ideas about a person or event in a particular way? If it is, the source's unbalanced view could be dangerous. If a historian accepts the information from a source like this as completely true, the version of history we have can become inaccurate and unreliable. On the other hand the source may represent the majority point of view of the time.

Decide how accurate the information in a source is. Ask yourself:
● What does the source tell us?
● What words or images in the source are used to put the subject in a good or bad light?
● Do we have any other sources with which we can check the accuracy of the source?
● What else do we know about the event or person being described in the source?
● Does this knowledge show the source to be trustworthy?

Decide, from what you know about the background of a source, how accurate it is. Ask yourself:
● When was it produced?
● Is it an interpretation? Is the author or artist trying to make us think about the past in a particular way?
● Was the author or artist present at the time of the event?
● What was the purpose of the writer or artist in producing the source?
● What information did the writer or artist put in, and what did he or she choose to leave out?
● What else do we know about how the author or artist arrived at this version of what happened?
● Was the author or artist expected to produce a balanced view?

POPULATION

KEY IDEAS

- Before 1801 population figures are unreliable

- The first census was in 1801

- The population rapidly increased because of a rising birth rate

- Britain was becoming urbanised

1. How and why was the size and distribution of Britain's population changing?

As you read through this book you will see that the rise in Britain's population had a part in many changes that took place. Source 3 shows how quickly Britain's population grew between 1751 and 1901 (Britain is made up of England, Wales and Scotland). The population nearly doubled in the 50 years after 1801, and then had nearly doubled again by 1900.

Britain's towns and cities grew with amazing speed (Source 4). This was not just because the total population grew. The most important factor was that the population shifted from town to country. This process is called urbanisation.

Studying changes in population is difficult for historians. Why?

2. How reliable are the figures used?

- The first national census (which counted the population) was not until 1801. For the years before that, historians have to use information from parish registers in which the priest recorded baptisms, marriages and burials. These records are not always accurate. Not all parish registers survive, and registers (or similar records) do not always exist for other denominations (such as Roman Catholics) or other religious groups (such as Jews).

- During the 18th century some writers tried to use what little information they could find to create a picture of the population. Gregory King used tax returns to produce figures for the size of the population, and the number of people doing certain jobs. His figures were only estimates.

Without a full census, it is difficult to know the size of the population, or at what point before 1801 it began to grow so rapidly. However, historians do have enough information to tell them that in 1751:

- Most people lived in the countryside.

- The south-east of England was the most populated part of Britain.

- London, Norwich and Bristol were the only three substantial cities.

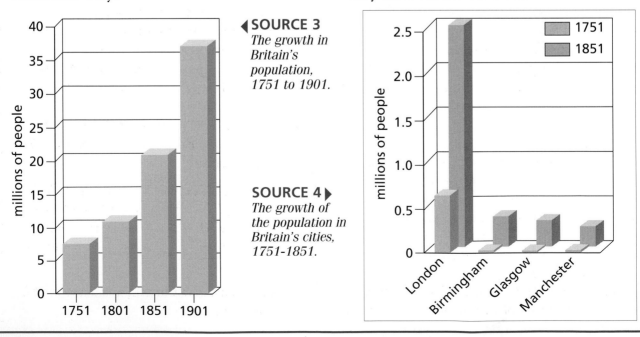

◀ **SOURCE 3**
The growth in Britain's population, 1751 to 1901.

SOURCE 4 ▶
The growth of the population in Britain's cities, 1751-1851.

3. Why did the population increase so rapidly?

Historians disagree about why the population increased. There are two theories:

The rising birth rate theory: (The birth rate is the number of babies born alive each year per 1,000 people in the total population.) This theory says that the birth rate was rising because the people were marrying earlier in life, and so women had more child-bearing years after their marriage. The reasons for earlier marriage were that:

● The Industrial Revolution provided more work and higher wages, so people could afford to marry earlier.

● Because of the shift from workshops to factories, fewer people served apprenticeships. An apprentice trained in a craft or trade for seven or nine years, and so did not have the income or freedom to marry young.

● The population was shifting to the towns from the countryside. People in the towns married as young as 20-years-old, while in the countryside people married at about 27-years-old. Figures show that in industrial Lancashire 40% of people between the ages of 17 and 30 were married, compared with 20% in rural areas.

The falling death rate theory: (The death rate is the number of deaths per 1,000 people in the population.) The reasons suggested for the falling death rate are that:

● Medical discoveries, like vaccinations against smallpox, were reducing the effects of killer diseases.

● The standard of hospitals and midwives was rising.

● Standards of living were improving.

There is not much evidence to support the death rate theory. The report of a survey in 1842 claimed that, on average, poor labourers living in Manchester died before the age of 17. Until the awareness of germs in 1864, diseases such as smallpox continued to be big killers. Hospitals were filthy until the later 19th century. Some historians are not convinced that standards of living were improving – most people lived in slums in both the town and countryside.

4. What were people's attitudes to the growth in population?

In 1798, the Reverend Thomas Malthus said that the population was growing too quickly. He warned that the country would not be able to produce enough food for everybody, unless people were persuaded to have fewer children. He suggested giving people low wages, so that they could not afford to marry. Malthus's ideas were criticised. In fact, the rising population resulted in increased production of food and manufactured products. It also provided the large numbers of workers that made the Industrial Revolution possible.

Questions

1. Why are population figures before 1801 so unreliable?

2. 'The cause of the growth of population in the 18th and 19th centuries was a rising birth rate, rather than a falling death rate.' Do you agree? Explain your answer.

3. Explain the attitude of the cartoonist in Source 5.

1 AGRICULTURE 1700 – 1815

1.1 How was the land organised in 1700?

In 1700 more people lived in the countryside than lived in towns or cities. The population of England and Wales was 5.5 million and over 80% (4.4 million) lived in villages. The village was the centre of the community. Farming was the main occupation and the craft workers in the village (such as weaver, blacksmith, and miller) were all dependent on agriculture.

The lives and work of the villagers were dominated by the seasons:

Spring: The fields were prepared for planting by teams of oxen or horses pulling heavy ploughs through the soil. A sower then walked along the strip **broadcasting** (throwing) seed, such as corn, to the left and right. A harrow, drawn by horses or oxen, followed the sower, dragging soil over the seeds to cover them.

Early summer: The grass in the hay meadow was cut and dried to make hay for cattle to eat in winter. Beekeepers collected honey, which was the only sweetening the villagers had. The sheep were washed and sheared. The days were long, so people spent a lot of time working.

Late summer: Farmers and labourers harvested the crops. They cut the corn with scythes and sickles, bound it into sheaves and left it to dry. When dry, the sheaves were loaded on to carts, taken to the farmyard and stacked into ricks.

Autumn: Most of the animals were killed because there was not enough fodder to feed them during the winter. Bacon joints were smoked over cottage fires, and pork and beef were pickled in tubs of salt water.

KEY IDEAS

- Most people lived in the countryside
- Fields were divided into strips
- There was a three-field crop rotation system
- Villagers had rights to the common land
- The population was low so the Open Field System worked

◄ **SOURCE 1**
A peasant harrowing with four oxen.

Winter: Crops were threshed (beaten) by hand to remove the hard husks from the grain ready for milling. The days were short, and lighting was expensive, so people could not work long hours.

These people were **subsistence farmers**. They grew and produced most of what they needed to live on. They had little in the way of spare produce to sell for money. Each family farmed a number of strips of land in the fields around their village. The villagers used a farming method called the **Open Field System**.

SOURCE 2
An 18th-century farmer.

9

What was the Open Field System?

Since the Middle Ages, most of England – especially the Midlands, East Anglia and the south – had been farmed using the Open Field System. A typical village contained three very large arable (crop growing) fields divided into **strips**. These were farmed by the villagers. There were no walls, hedges or fences to separate the land. The strips were separated by grassy banks called '**balks**'. These balks were never ploughed, and all kinds of rough grass and weeds grew on them. The size of the strips varied greatly, but most were about 200 metres long and 20 metres wide. The villagers each owned a different number of strips depending on their social position. Their strips were scattered throughout the three fields so that they would each have their share of good and bad land.

Growing corn and barley took the goodness (the nutrients) from the soil. To keep the fields fertile the villagers rotated their crops – no crop was grown in the same field two years running. As people did not know about fertilisers, one field in three was left **fallow** (no crops were planted) each year. This was so the land would regain its nutrients. Weeds grew on the fallow field and animals ate the weeds. Manure from the animals was a natural fertiliser. The table below shows how the crop rotation was organised.

	Field 1	Field 2	Field 3
Year 1	Corn	Fallow	Barley
Year 2	Barley	Corn	Fallow
Year 3	Fallow	Barley	Corn

Around the village was the **common land**. All the villagers had rights to this land. They could use it for grazing their animals, collecting firewood and berries. Poor farmers (squatters) built huts on the common and lived there for free.

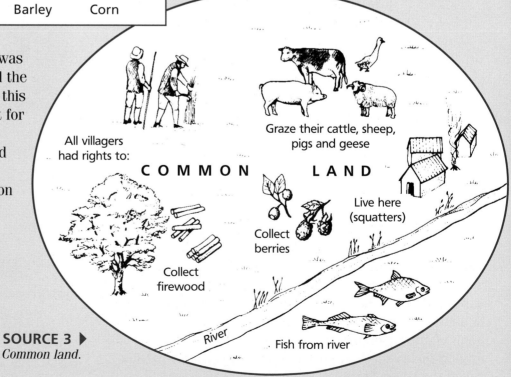

All villagers had rights to:

COMMON LAND

Graze their cattle, sheep, pigs and geese

Live here (squatters)

Collect berries

Collect firewood

River

Fish from river

SOURCE 3 ▶
Common land.

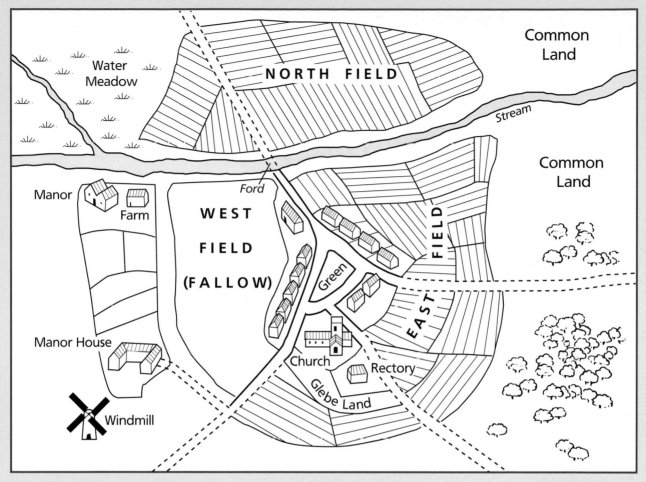

SOURCE 4 ▲
An Open Field Village.

Why did the Open Field System last so long?

The Open Field System created a strong **community spirit** – the villagers all worked together sharing tools and equipment. They could use the common land to supplement their needs. This system of farming was traditional – it had been used for over 600 years. The system had lasted so long because it provided the village with nearly all its basic needs. Most farmers were reluctant to change and preferred to use the traditional ways. Some farmers did favour new methods of farming, but they knew that they would meet with opposition. One such farmer thought that people would reject all ideas of change by saying, *'Away with your fool Notions, there are too many Bees in your Bonnett case, we will satisfy ourselves with such measures as our fathers have followed hitherto'.*

The Open Field System enabled farmers to grow just enough to live on. Because the population of England had remained low, and only changed very slowly over the centuries, there was no need to produce extra food. However, from about 1750 onwards, the population began to grow rapidly. In fact, it grew by $3^1/2$ million between about 1700 and 1800. More food was needed to feed the extra population. The Open Field System was unable to produce more food to meet this increasing demand.

1.2 Why could the Open Field System not feed the growing population?

KEY IDEAS

Disadvantages of the Open Field System:

- Land was wasted

- No selective animal breeding

- Broadcast sowing wasted seed

- Time was wasted walking between strips

- It was impossible to experiment

The Open Field System did not make the best use of resources.

Land was wasted

- One field out of three was left fallow each year to give the soil a chance to recover. Therefore one-third of the arable land was wasted each year.

- The common land was an area which could have been farmed.

- The balks separating the strips of land took up space which could have been used to cultivate crops.

Poor quality animals

- Animals often wandered over the open fields trampling and eating the crops.

- Healthy and diseased animals grazed together, so disease was easily spread. Liver fluke and foot rot in sheep, and cattle plague were common diseases.

- Selective breeding was impossible because animals were not penned in. When strong and weak animals mated, overall quality suffered.

- There were too many animals for the grass on the land. Animals were often thin.

- Most animals had to be slaughtered in the autumn because not enough fodder was produced to feed them through the winter. The ones that were kept alive were even thinner by the spring.

Seed was wasted

Seed was sown using the broadcast method. A sower had a basket of seed hung around his neck. He would scatter handfuls on to the strip as

SOURCE 5 ▶
Sheep. (Compare this picture to Source 25 on page 25.)

12

◀ **SOURCE 6**
*A broadcast
sower.*

Increased demand

The Open Field System had always been wasteful, but this had not mattered when the population was low. As the population began to grow, a more efficient method of farming was needed.

Thomas Malthus, a clergyman, published a book in 1798 entitled *An Essay on The Principles of Population*. In it he predicted a shortage of agricultural land. He warned that disease and famine would follow if nothing was done to stop the population explosion.

The population grew even more quickly than Malthus had predicted, but fortunately his gloomy forecast did not come true. Improved farming methods enabled Britain to feed its growing population. **Enclosure** was an important reason for this.

he walked along, but a lot of seed ended up being wasted. In some spots there was too much seed. The harrow did not cover all the seed with soil. Any seed left uncovered was then eaten by birds. Some seed landed on the balks and not on the strips.

Time was wasted

The farmers' houses and cottages were clustered around the centre of the village. A farmer had to walk a long way to reach all his strips in the different fields. One farmer complained, *'I have 23 strips in the fields nearly two miles from home. I spend too much time running around the village instead of farming my land'.*

No opportunities for experimentation

The Open Field System was a traditional method of farming. It was a communal system. Villagers had to sow, plough and harvest their crops at the same time. This made it impossible to experiment with new ideas because everybody had to work at the same pace.

Questions

1. What do you understand by 'subsistence farming' (page 9)?

2. Look at Source 4, an Open Field Village, (page 11). What does this source show you about the way farming was organised under the Open Field System?

3. Give the three ways in which the common land was valuable to the villagers. (See page 10.)

4. Give three reasons why the Open Field System had lasted so long (page 11).

5 Draw a diagram to show the disadvantages of the Open Field System.

1.3 *What were the causes of enclosure* ?

One of the great changes that took place in agriculture during the 18th century was the rapid increase in the number of '**enclosures**'. Whole parishes or particular districts changed from strip farming, open fields and common land, to enclosures. These were fields surrounded by a hedge, fence or wall. This sort of field was smaller than the open field. Each enclosure only had one owner.

Enclosures had been used since the 16th century for sheep farming, but in the second-half of the 18th century there was an unusually rapid increase in the number of enclosures. Permission for enclosure was usually given by Act of Parliament. By looking at the number of Enclosure Acts that were passed you can see how the number of enclosures increased between 1730 and 1815.

KEY IDEAS

- Growing demand for food led to enclosure
- Farmers saw the chance to make profits
- Most Enclosure Acts were made during the French Wars
- Farmers wanted to experiment with new ideas

Years	Number of Enclosure Acts passed
1730 – 1759	212
1760 – 1789	1,291
1790 – 1815	2,144

SOURCE 7
Causes of enclosure. ▼

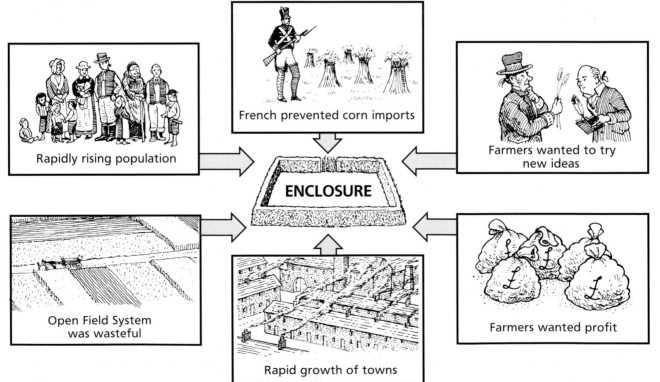

Rapidly rising population

French prevented corn imports

Farmers wanted to try new ideas

ENCLOSURE

Open Field System was wasteful

Rapid growth of towns

Farmers wanted profit

From Source 7 it can be seen that there were a number of reasons why the open fields were gradually replaced by enclosures.

◄ **SOURCE 8**
The Battle of Waterloo which finally ended the French wars in 1815.

Growth of population

The population was growing rapidly. In 1760 the estimated population of England and Wales was 6.7 million and by the first census in 1801 it had risen to 9.3 million. More food was needed to feed these 2.6 million extra people. As we have seen, the Open Field System was too wasteful to produce more food. Enclosure, on the other hand, could increase crop yields, produce better livestock and provide more food for the country.

Growth of industrial towns

As the population grew, people were also moving from the countryside to find work in the growing industrial towns. Towns, such as Liverpool, Manchester and Birmingham, expanded rapidly to contain the large labour force needed by the new textile, iron and coal industries. These workers had to buy food brought in from the countryside.

This growing market for food in the towns encouraged farmers to produce more. As transport improved, they could send perishable produce away to the towns instead of having to sell it locally. It was a chance for farmers to make profits from their land.

Experimentation with new ideas

As the owners of successful new industries grew richer, they bought country estates. They invested a lot of their capital in the land, and wanted to use new and more productive methods. On enclosed land they could experiment with new crop rotations, they could use new machinery and practice selective breeding. New methods meant more efficient farming, better crops and livestock, and higher profits for farmers.

The French Wars

Another major reason for enclosures was the French Wars. From 1793-1815 Britain was almost continually at war with France. Britain had relied on imported corn to supplement home supplies. France hoped to starve Britain into surrender by blockading the English Channel to prevent imports of corn.

As this meant corn was in short supply the prices rose. Farmers wanted to enclose more land (including the common land) to grow more corn so that Britain could be self-sufficient. But as there was no competition from abroad, farmers also saw the opportunity to charge high prices and make large profits.

Questions

1. What do you understand by the word 'enclosure'?

2. During which period were most Enclosure Acts passed? Why?

3. Which of the following was the most important reason for the introduction of enclosures before 1815:
   (a) the growth of population;
   (b) the French Wars 1793-1815;
   (c) the growth of industrial towns; or
   (d) farmers wanting to increase profits?
   Explain your answer carefully by referring to what you have read in this section.

1.4 How was enclosure achieved ?

There were three ways that permission for enclosure could be obtained:

- By consent of all the landowners in the village.
- By one man buying all the land in the open fields.
- By Act of Parliament.

Between 1700 and 1813 one-third of England's parishes were enclosed. This was about 8 million acres. Of that area around 5½ million acres were enclosed by Act of Parliament and nearly 2½ million acres by private agreement.

How people applied for an Act of Enclosure

- A public meeting was called, usually by the biggest landowner, and attended by all the landowners in the village.
- If the owners of four-fifths of the land agreed to enclosure, a request to enclose the village was sent to Parliament asking for an Enclosure Act.
- Parliament was usually willing to pass the Act because most MPs came from large landowning families and supported enclosure.
- A notice was pinned to the local church door, informing villagers that there was going to be enclosure. Villagers could protest if they wished.
- Once the Act was passed, three or five Commissioners were appointed by Parliament to draw up the enclosure. They were sent to the village to check on everyone's legal right

to the land. The common land and waste land were also included in the enclosure. When the open fields were being enclosed, the land was divided up with people given ownership of one or more enclosed fields. The Commissioners worked out what each landowner was entitled to (the Enclosure Award) and they sorted out disputes. The Commissioners appointed surveyors and valuers to plan the new fields and roads in the village, as illustrated in Source 9.

KEY IDEAS

- Most land was enclosed by Act of Parliament
- Large landowners often influenced the enclosure decision
- Common land and waste land were included in enclosure
- Commissioners were appointed to reallocate the land
- Surveyors planned new fields and roads

SOURCE 9
Surveyors at work in the open fields. ▼

Who suffered and who benefited in the process of Parliamentary Enclosure?

The poorer villagers (cottagers) suffered as a result of this procedure. Their opinions were not taken into account. Cottagers had problems if they could not show the Commissioners written proof of which strips of land they owned. Many cottagers did not have these documents because the land had been passed down in the family for generations. When the Enclosure Award was made, many small landowners were unable to afford the legal costs and expenses of the commissioners and surveyors for having their land enclosed.

Villagers who owned no land often did not know anything was happening until the Act of Enclosure was passed. In theory, villagers could dispute the Enclosure Award, but in practice this was not easy. People who could not write (and most people could not) were unable to take up a dispute because it had to be done in writing. The costs involved in a dispute, such as travelling to London and

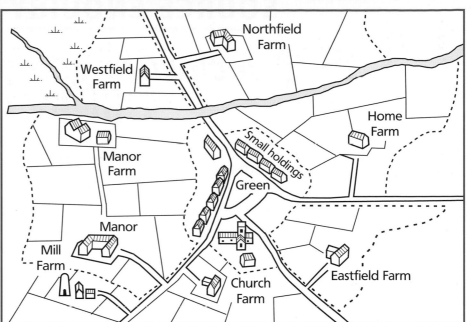

SOURCE 10
An enclosed village. ▲

hiring lawyers, were also too high for most villagers.

The large landowners got what they wanted because they could afford the costs of enclosure (Source 11). Many landowners had friends and family who were MPs so it was fairly easy to get Acts passed. Once the Commissioners arrived in the village, the large landowners had little trouble in establishing a claim to the best land, often through bribery – this might be by simply arranging for the Commissioners to have free board and lodgings during their stay.

	£
Legal charges	876
Parliamentary expenses	219
Commissioners' fees	1,284
Commissioners' expenses	251
Surveyors' fees	934
Roads and paths	1,030
Stakes and fences	184
Miscellaneous	916
TOTAL	5,694

SOURCE 11
The costs of enclosing land in Sheffield. ▲

Questions

1. Draw a diagram to show the stages of enclosure by Act of Parliament.

2. Look at Source 9. What are the men doing in the picture? Briefly explain why they are doing this job.

3. Look at Source 11. What does this source show you about the costs of enclosure in the late 18th century?

1.5 *Was enclosure good or bad* ?

Who suffered from enclosure?

● **The community spirit** of the village broke down as people moved from the centre of the village to live in the new farmhouses built alongside their land. They no longer worked together, sharing tools as they had done under the Open Field System.

● Many **small farmers** found it difficult to compete with the richer farmers who could afford to buy the latest machinery, and to pay for having their land drained and manured. They often could not afford the costs of enclosure, and had to sell their land to the larger landowners. Some became tenant farmers, paying high rents to landowners. Some worked as labourers on the new farms. Others moved to a town.

● Even if the **cottagers** had proof of the land they owned they were usually given the least fertile land after enclosure. Often they found that they could not afford to pay for the compulsory fencing.

● Possibly the greatest hardship caused by enclosure was the loss of the common land. Because this land was made into fields, it was no longer free for everyone to use. The **squatters**, who had lived there were forced off the common land and often moved to the towns. Poorer families had relied on the common land for feeding their animals, and collecting firewood.

> ### KEY IDEAS
> ● Community spirit often broke down
>
> ● Villagers lost rights to the common land
>
> ● People moved to the towns to find work
>
> ● More food was produced for the growing population
>
> ● Farmers could use new methods
>
> ● More profit was made and reinvested into the land

Many of these people gave up trying to support themselves and went on Poor Relief (see pages 124-127).

Clearly enclosure caused a great upheaval in the lives of many squatters, labourers and cottagers. But the lowest farming classes had never been well off. Even if enclosure had not happened, the rise in population would have caused hardship, and there would still have been unemployment.

SOURCE 12 ▶
Extract from a Board of Agriculture Report written in 1808:

The common was very extensive. I spoke with a farmer who said that enclosure would ruin England; it was worse than ten wars. 'Why, my friend, what have you lost by it?' 'I kept four cows before the parish was enclosed and now I don't keep so much as a goose.'

Who gained from enclosure?

● **The large landowners** knew they could benefit from enclosure – which was why they promoted the idea. To go through the process of enclosure, and to invest in new farming methods, required money. The large landowners could afford these costs. They

SOURCE 13 ▶
Arthur Young wrote down what he saw when he rode around England in 1770:

I must note the amazing profits made from wool in enclosed districts compared with areas that have open fields. In the Vale of Evesham, the average fleece is about 9 pounds weight in the enclosures but only 3 pounds in the open fields.

bought cheap land off the smaller farmers, and charged high rents to tenant farmers. They invested in new machinery, such as Jethro Tull's Seed Drill. They experimented with Townshend's Norfolk Four-Course Crop Rotation. They practised selective breeding, resulting in heavier, healthier animals which sold for a higher price. In fact, between the beginning and end of the 18th century, farmers improved their methods so much that the total output on farms increased by 500%. As the possibility of making a profit became increasingly apparent, rich men were willing to invest their capital (money) in farming.

● In the long run **everyone** gained from enclosure. Enclosed farms provided extra employment in hedging, fencing and ditching. There were also new roads to build and farmhouses to construct. Villagers who found

work after enclosure often had higher wages and a better standard of living than before.

There was more land under cultivation which grew more food for the rapidly growing population. During the French Wars enclosure allowed more food to be produced, which compensated for the lack of imports at that time. Farmers were able to distribute their produce longer distances due to improvements in transport. They could now sell their produce to the population in the growing towns.

The diet of the population improved as the new farming methods produced a wider variety of crops and an increased availability of fresh meat. People were healthier, and they lived longer.

SOURCE 14
Covent Garden in the early 19th century, selling a variety of fruits and vegetables. ▼

SOURCE ENQUIRY

In the 18th and 19th centuries many people were interested in recording the world around them. People who wanted to make their opinions known, like Arthur Young, often had their thoughts printed and distributed to other interested people. This provides very useful evidence for historians who want to understand the past.

BENEFITS TO AGRICULTURE

SOURCE 15

A conversation at Fairfield, Northamptonshire. A summer evening in 1785. Six villagers are talking outside the churchyard on their way home from the open fields.

John Pidney (*removing a straw from his mouth*): It don't seem loikly do it? No more corn and hens for the parson. He's got to have his tithes in money now.

Peter Haystack (*scratching himself*): Ay, Oi reckon E's mad at it. E don't loike the idea o' money, says it can alter. Some year it'll buy less goods than others. But a load o' wheat – that's allus the same.

Jake Smith (*leaning forward from the church wall and speaking angrily*): And he's not the only one that's mad at these enclosures. He'll get his tithes, and his glebe land is safe enough. But what about me? Had cheeky devil of a commissioner round last night asking for a copy of me deed to the three acres I hev' in the West and East Fields. I've got no deed – don't need none, I told him. Me father an' his father afore him farmed that land and it'll take more than a city gent loike him to move me off it. You were no good friend to this village, Peter Johnson, agreeing with the squire that we should have enclosures.

John Pidup: Aye, he's right, Pete. What did yer want to do that for, eh?

Peter Johnson (*standing with his legs apart and pointing fiercely at Jake Smith*): What the devil are you talking about? I've been asking at village court every solid year for last ten years whether I could get me strips together. No – I've to do what the rest of you do. And none of you want to move with the times. What good was it Mr Arthur Young coming to 'The Dog and Partridge' to tell us about turnips when none of you will plant em? There's money to be made – and I want to make it. Look at them miserable, scabby beasts on the common. Half my cattle die every year because they mix with such maggoty creatures. I want to get some o' Mr Bakewell's New Leicestershires. I'll make your eyes open, you've never sin such sheep. But they're not for that common.

Martin Thatcher (*a small thin man*): Aye – but what about us poor cottagers? What will happen to us? We've got no land in the fields. What will I do if I can't put me cow on the common?

Peter Johnson: There'll be plenty o' work for you, Martin. I'll need men to put up hedges and weed between me new crops. Then there'll be roads to be made – no more o' these muddy tracks for Fairfield. There'll be plenty o' work for all.

SOURCE 16

In 1813, Arthur Young wrote, in General View of the Agriculture of the County of Lincoln: ▼

The vast benefit of enclosing can, upon inferior soils, be rarely seen in more advantageous light than upon Lincoln-heath. I found a large piece of common land which formerly was covered with heath, gorse etc., and yielding in fact little or no produce, converted by enclosure into profitable arable farms; let on average of 10s an acre, and a very extensive countryside, all studded with new farmhouses, barns, offices, and every appearance of thriving industry ... rents have risen on the heath ... the farmers are in much better circumstances, a great produce is created, cattle and sheep increased, and the poor employed ...

SOURCE 17 ▼

A tenant farmer, who lost his own land in enclosure, now pays rent to his new landlord.

SOURCE 18 ▼

Arthur Young was a failed farmer and agricultural journalist. He rode around England making notes about the effects of enclosure:

What it is to the poor man to be told that the Houses of Parliament are very concerned about his property, while the father of the family is forced to sell his cow and his land because he can't own one without the other: and being deprived of his incentive to work, spends his money, gets into bad habits, enlists for a soldier and leaves his wife and children to the parish? The poor in these parishes may say and with truth, 'Parliament may be tender of property; all I know is, I had a cow, and an Act of Parliament has taken it from me'.

SOURCE 19 ▼

F. Moore wrote, in Considerations on the Exorbitant Price of Proprietors, *1773:*

In passing through a village near Swaffham ... I beheld the houses tumbling into ruins, and the common fields all enclosed ... I was informed that a gentleman of Lynn had bought that township and the next adjoining to it: that he had thrown the one into three, and the other into four farms; which before the enclosure were in about twenty farms: and upon my further enquiring what was becoming to the farmers who were turned out, the answer was that some of them were dead and the rest were become labourers.

FARMERS LOSE LAND

Questions

1. Read Source 16. How had enclosure benefited the County of Lincoln?

2. Are the reasons given in Source 16 the only benefits of enclosure in the late 18th and early 19th centuries?

3. Read Sources 12, 18 and 19. What are the main arguments against enclosure? Which two of these sources agree the most about the problems with enclosure? Explain your answer with reference to the sources.

4. Study Source 17. What can you learn about the effects of enclosure from this source?

5. Read Source 15. These men have different opinions on the effects of enclosure. What reasons can you give to explain this? Explain your answer with reference to the source and the text.

6. Using the evidence in the text and the sources, write a letter to a fellow landlord explaining why you believe he should support your plan to enclose the village in which you are both big landowners.

1.6 What were the new ideas and methods for increasing production?

The farmers who had thought traditional methods still worked well, were soon proved wrong. The enclosed farms, using improved machinery, new crop rotations and selective breeding, produced greater yields.

Better machinery

Jethro Tull (1674-1741), a Berkshire farmer, published a book in 1731 called *Horse Hoeing Husbandry*. In it he described the development of two farming tools, the **Horse-Drawn Seed Drill** for sowing seeds and the **Horse-Drawn Hoe** for weeding the fields. The Seed Drill planted seeds evenly in rows and a harrow at

KEY IDEAS

- Jethro Tull invented the Seed Drill and the Horse Drawn Hoe

- The Norfolk Four Course Crop Rotation removed the need for the fallow field

- Selective breeding increased the weight of animals

SOURCE 20

It was very difficult to find a man that could sow clover well; they had a habit to throw it once with the hand to two large strides – thus with 9 or 10lb of seed to an acre, two-thirds of the ground was unplanted. To remedy this I made a hopper, to be pulled by a boy, that planted an acre sufficiently with 6lbs of seed; but when I added to this an exceedingly light plough that made 6 channels eight inches apart, into which 2lbs to an acre being drilled, the ground was well planted.

An extract from Horse Hoeing Husbandry *by Jethro Tull.*

SOURCE 21
Lord Townshend ('Turnip' Townshend). ▼

the back of the machine covered the seeds with soil. It was a great improvement on the old broadcast method – a lot of seed was saved and output increased. Tull even claimed that using the Seed Drill could produce double the crops for a third less seed (but this was never proved).

Although these machines were important developments the seed drill often broke down and was not used for over a hundred years after its invention. The Horse-Drawn Hoe was also an advancement that farmers were slow to appreciate. Farmers at the time regarded Tull as rather eccentric. (This was mainly because he did not understand the importance of manuring land.) Although Tull's book helped spread his ideas it was only of limited use as many people could not read.

Improved crop rotations

In 1730 **Lord Townshend** (1670-1738) realised that his political career was over after he had a row with the Prime Minister, Sir Robert Walpole. He then swapped politics for the challenges of farming his estates at Raynham, Norfolk.

Norfolk had poor and sandy soil so Townshend used a mixture of clay and lime (called **marl**) to fertilise the soil and so produce better crops. He followed the Dutch example of growing turnips and clover in the fields instead of leaving land fallow (which had been so wasteful in the Open Field System). Sets of four fields were usually used, and – in a typical cycle – corn, turnips, clover and barley were alternated. The turnips helped to clean the ground of weeds. Animals could be put in the field and while they ate the turnip tops they enriched the soil with their manure. Clover was also used for animal fodder but, very importantly, it gave off nitrogen. This fertilised the soil and made it richer for growing crops.

Townshend made this crop rotation method popular among farmers, and it became known as the **Norfolk Four-Course Crop Rotation**. (Source 22 shows how the Rotation worked if four fields were used.)

The Norfolk Four-Course Crop Rotation had very important results.
- No land was left fallow, every field was cultivated.
- More crops were produced from the same amount of land. Therefore more food was provided for the growing population.
- The turnips and clover were used as additional winter fodder for animals, so there was no longer any need to slaughter so many of them in the autumn.
- Animal dung was used to manure the fields.
- The people had a healthier diet, as now fresh meat was available throughout the year.

Townshend's ideas were followed more quickly than Tull's. Because he had been a public figure in Parliament, he got much more publicity for his methods. However, the spread of new ideas was still held back because many farmers were reluctant to change from their traditional ways.

SOURCE 22
Norfolk Four-Course Crop Rotation. ▼

	Field 1	Field 2	Field 3	Field 4
Year 1	Corn	Turnips	Barley	Clover
Year 2	Clover	Corn	Turnips	Barley
Year 3	Barley	Clover	Corn	Turnips
Year 4	Turnips	Barley	Clover	Corn

Selective breeding of animals

The increased use of enclosures, and production of winter fodder as a result of Townshend's Norfolk Four-Course Crop Rotation, meant that improvements could now be made in rearing livestock. Under the Open Field System, animals were underweight, often diseased, and there was no control over their breeding. At the time a farmer complained, *'I want to buy some of Mr Bakewell's New Leicester Sheep but it is useless doing so if they have to graze on the common with all the scabbed lousy, maggoty beasts in the neighbourhood, for they will soon be eaten with maggots too'.*

Robert Bakewell (1725-1795), a Leicestershire farmer, was interested in breeding animals and is most famous for two high quality breeds, the **'Longhorn Cattle'** and **'New Leicestershire Sheep'** (Sources 24 and 25).

By using selective breeding he was able to produce sheep and cattle with shorter legs, smaller bones and barrel-shaped bodies. This resulted in more meat, and therefore in more profit for farmers. He also ensured that his animals were healthy and properly fed. He kept detailed notes on how quickly the animals grew, the amount of meat on them, and the quantity and the quality of wool on the sheep. His animals improved visibly in each successive generation until, in a short space of time, heavier and better-shaped animals were being produced.

The results of Bakewell's work were very important.

● Animal weights increased:

▼ SOURCE 23
Robert Bakewell.

SOURCE 24
One of Bakewell's improved Longhorn cattle. ▲

	1700	1800
Lambs	8 kg	23 kg
Sheep	13 kg	36 kg
Calves	23 kg	64 kg
Cattle	176 kg	365 kg

24

SOURCE 25 ▲

Rams bred on Bakewell's farm were hired by other farmers to mate with their ewes. This meant that flocks around the country improved. Look back at Source 5 on page 12 to see how sheep had improved.

● Animal husbandry became profitable. For example, in 1760 Bakewell charged 16s (80p) a season for the use of his rams to mate with ewes, but by 1786 he could pick and choose his clients, and rented out rams at 400 guineas (£420) for a third of the season. (This was 1,575 times more than he charged before.)

● By rearing bigger animals, Bakewell had shown how the demand for more meat in the growing towns could be met. A greater availability of fresh meat resulted in the people having a healthier diet.

His work was soon followed and improved upon by others. The Colling Brothers of County Durham adopted Bakewell's ideas and developed Shorthorn Cattle. Some thought that Bakewell's animals were too fatty to please rich people. The Colling Brothers bred lean animals, insisted on good pedigrees and were able to charge a higher price for their cattle.

Questions

1. Read Source 20. What is the name of the traditional method of sowing seeds described here? What is Tull's main criticism of this method?

2. Draw a chart to illustrate the advantages of the Norfolk Four-Course Crop Rotation.

3. How did the organisation of the Norfolk Four-Course Crop Rotation differ from that of the Three Field System?

4. Study Source 25. What does this source tell you about the condition of animals on Bakewell's farm?

5. Draw a graph to show the increased weight of animals as a result of Bakewell's selective breeding.

6. The following led to agricultural improvements:
   (a) Lord Townshend's Norfolk Four-Course Crop Rotation;
   (b) Jethro Tull's Seed Drill;
   (c) Robert Bakewell's Selective Breeding.

   Were any of these more important than the others?

   Explain your answer fully by referring to each improvement.

1.7 How did new agricultural ideas spread?

How would a farmer in Devon know about Bakewell's work with animals many miles away in Leicestershire? There were various ways of spreading information. For example, news was spread by the written word, by people attending agricultural fairs and shows, and through information from the newly-formed Board of Agriculture.

Arthur Young (1741-1820) was an important promoter of new ideas. His small farm had failed, but because he was so enthusiastic about the new methods, he became an agricultural journalist. He travelled through England and wrote detailed descriptions of the farming methods he saw. He was strongly in favour of large farms and the Norfolk Four-Course Crop Rotation. However, he admitted that the poor suffered from enclosure. From 1784 he edited the *Annals of Agriculture*. This journal contained articles on the latest farming ideas, including some by **King George III** (1738-1820) who used the pen name 'Ralph Robinson'. George III used many of the improvements on his farm in Windsor Park and was nicknamed 'Farmer George'.

In 1793 the **Board of Agriculture** was set up, partly supported by the Government, with Arthur Young as its Secretary. The aim was to investigate and stimulate new ideas in farming, so that more food would be produced, because the French Wars had just broken out. Under Arthur Young's direction, a complete survey of the farming resources of England was carried out, and a volume was published about each county. The Board was

> ## KEY IDEAS
>
> Ideas were spread by:
>
> - Young's *Annals of Agriculture*
> - Coke's Sheep Shearing Meetings
> - the Board of Agriculture
>
> Change was slow because of :
>
> - poor communications
> - farmers' resistance to change

SOURCE 26 ▲
Woburn Sheep-Shearing Festival, 1811.

useful in spreading ideas and offered advice on a wide range of subjects including drainage and animal feed.

Thomas Coke (1754-1842), was a wealthy farmer who had large estates at Holkham, Norfolk. He was a great advocate of the new farming methods, and promoted their use on his estates. He added marl and manure to the sandy soil to improve its quality. He used a Seed Drill and the Norfolk Four-Course Crop Rotation. He became well known for breeding animals, especially Southdown Sheep and Devon Cattle. He gave his tenants long leases at fixed rents to encourage them to use the new methods on their land.

From 1778 onwards he held annual sheep-shearing meetings known locally as 'Coke's Clippings'. This was a very important way of advertising the latest trends in farming. Visitors could view the new farming implements and improved breeds, and swap ideas. Soon visitors came from all over Britain and some from continental Europe. By 1815 the meetings attracted over 5,000 people. Other wealthy farmers, including the Duke of Bedford at Woburn Abbey (see Source 26), copied Coke's idea and held sheep shearings.

Why didn't new ideas spread quickly?

Arthur Young wrote some very useful and interesting farming articles. But, in spite of the work of Young and others, new ideas did not spread quickly. Methods of communication in the farming community were poor. Not everybody could read. Many farmers clung to old methods because they were reluctant to change. Other landowners were reluctant to invest in new systems that encouraged change, such as giving tenants long leases.

All these changes in farming formed part of the '**Agricultural Revolution**'. Although the changes were slow and patchy, the effects were vitally important. The improvements

SOURCE 28 ▲
Arthur Young.

in farming methods, that brought about enclosures, higher yields and better livestock, enabled Britain to feed the growing population and provided money for investment into other areas of the economy, including industry and transport.

SOURCE 27

Arthur Young noted how Lord Rockingham wanted to improve the cultivation of turnips and introduce hoeing on his estates at Wentworth, South Yorkshire:

With this view he attempted to persuade his tenants to come into the method, described the operations, pointed out its advantages, clearly explained the great consequence of increasing the size of the roots … yet with a set of men of fixed ideas, used to a stated road, with turns neither to the right nor left, it had very little effect: turnips continued to be sown, but were never hoed.

Questions

1. Study Source 26. Why were agricultural festivals like this so important?

2. Draw a diagram to show all the ways of spreading the new ideas in the late 18th and early 19th centuries.

3. Read Source 27. What did Lord Rockingham hope to introduce? Why was he unable to do so? What reason could you give to explain the attitude of his tenants?

4. Why were the methods used to spread new farming ideas not always successful?

2 AGRICULTURE 1815 – 1900

2.1 *How did people react to agricultural change up to 1840*

During the French Wars (1793-1815) many small land owners and tenant farmers had managed to live comfortably, due to the high prices that they could charge for their corn. However, after the wars ended, there was more competition from abroad. Corn prices dropped, and many farms went out of business. Then in early 1815 the Government introduced the **Corn Laws**, an import restriction, on grain coming into Britain. Corn prices (and therefore the price of bread) rose again. Bread was the staple diet of most people, but some could not afford it.

Life was hard at this time for cottagers and squatters. They were forced to move as a result of enclosure. Although many found jobs as farm labourers these were not secure. They were often employed day to day, or at best week to week and no work meant no pay. Frequently labourers' weekly outgoings were more than their wages. Many labourers at this time lived in real poverty, and in very primitive accommodation (Source 1). A man, wife and perhaps ten children could be living in a two-roomed cottage. A Poor Law official from Ampthill in Bedfordshire described the labourers' cottages as, *'very miserable places in which it is impossible to keep up the common decencies of life'*.

Labourers living in the south of England suffered the most. Their wages were low, and they often could not afford to feed themselves or their families. During the 1820s dissatisfaction among the labouring classes increased. Bad harvests in 1828 and 1829 made their situation even worse. Increasing numbers of labourers felt, not only that they were underpaid, but that their jobs were threatened by the introduction of new machines.

The labourers had always worked in the winter, threshing the autumn-harvested crops by hand. However, by the 1820s most wealthy farmers had bought threshing machines which did the work much faster. Without this seasonal employment, labourers faced severe poverty and unemployment, but landlords and wealthy farmers ignored their protests.

SOURCE 1 ▲
The interior of a labourer's cottage at Blandford, Dorset drawn by an Illustrated London News *artist in about 1840.*

The Swing Riots

In the summer of 1830, riots broke out in Kent, and soon spread across the south of England. Farm labourers banded together and went around farms demanding the destruction of the threshing machines, and an increase in wages. If the farmers refused, the men threatened to smash their threshing machines, set fire to their hayricks and burn down barns full of corn. The demands to the landowners were signed with the name of a fictional 'Captain Swing' (see Source 2). The riots became known as the 'Swing Riots'. The Government reacted strongly. Nine workers were hanged, and 450 were transported to Australia.

After the riots failed, some farm labourers moved to the towns or emigrated, hoping for a better life. It cannot have been easy for people with no knowledge or experience of anything except farming to suddenly leave everything they knew behind. It was not until after 1840 that the conditions of farm labourers gradually improved.

This is to inform you what you have to undergo gentlemen if you don't pull down your messhines and rise the poor men's wages or we will burn down your barns and you in them.

This is the last notis.

from Swing

◀ **SOURCE 2**
A letter sent to a farmer, signed by 'Captain Swing'. (The person who wrote this was not good at spelling.)

2.2 Why were the Corn Laws introduced and why were they repealed?

In the 18th century, it was normal practice for the Government to place restrictions on trade – such as customs duties on goods entering or leaving the country. Sometimes this was to raise money. Sometimes it was to control trade. If it was to protect the interests of British producers it was referred to as 'protectionism'. In 1776, Adam Smith wrote *The Wealth of Nations,* advocating the idea of free trade (trading without any duties). He believed that Government should not control trade, and so customs duties should be abolished.

Why were the Corn Laws introduced in 1815?

Farmers and large landowners did not share Smith's views on free trade. They had prospered during the French Wars when there was no competition from abroad, and corn prices were high. When the wars ended in 1815, and imports began again, British farmers were afraid that their profits would drop. They asked Parliament to pass the Corn Laws to protect them from foreign competition.

The Corn Laws prohibited the import of corn into Britain until the price of British corn had reached a certain level (80s – £4 – a quarter). This was unpopular with the public. In March 1815 mobs protested in London fearing the Laws would mean dearer bread (Source 3). However, the Corn Laws were passed in March 1815, because most MPs' income came from land and they were keen to protect their interests. For 'free traders' the Corn Laws symbolised the protectionism they wanted to abolish.

SOURCE 3
Crowds protesting against the Corn Laws, 1815. ▲

Why were the Corn Laws repealed in 1846?

The movement for free trade revived in the 1820s. Manufacturers in the expanding industries such as cotton, pottery and iron felt sure that they could sell their goods in the world market. William Huskisson, MP for Liverpool and President of the Board of Trade, removed many duties on imports of

The **Anti-Corn Law League** (ACLL) was formed in Manchester, in 1839, by industrialists and merchants who wanted free trade. They believed that the Corn Laws were responsible for a depression in trade in the late 1830s. They thought that trade could only grow if all barriers and restrictions were removed. Factory owners were also suffering because their workers were demanding higher wages so that they could afford the high cost of bread. The ACLL started a very well-organised campaign to have the Corn Laws repealed. Members thought that it was unfair to protect farmers from foreign imports of corn while manufacturers had to compete on the world markets. They also argued that foreigners would not buy British goods if Britain refused to buy imported corn.

raw materials and consumer goods. He also relaxed the Navigation Laws to give the British colonies greater freedom to trade directly with other nations. He realised that the fixed price for corn of 80s per quarter was too high, so in 1828 he imposed a sliding scale of duties for corn.

Landowners opposed Huskisson's measure and he was forced to resign. However, this sliding scale made little difference to the price of bread which was still high.

SOURCE 4 ▲
Starving families attack a potato store.

SOURCE 5

In 1841, Richard Cobden spoke against the Corn Laws in the first speech he ever made in the House of Commons:

He had heard that tax called by a multitude of names. Some designated it as a 'protection'; but it was a tax after all, and he would call it nothing else. The bread tax was levied principally upon the working classes ... It compelled the working classes to pay 40 per cent more, that is, a higher price than they should pay if there was a free trade in corn ...

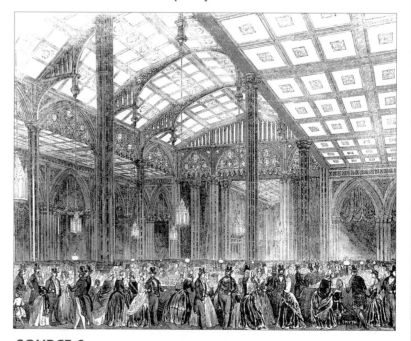

SOURCE 6 ▲
An Anti-Corn Law League bazaar, Theatre Royal, Covent Garden, 1845. It was organised by a committee of 'one thousand ladies'.

Why was the ACLL successful?

- It was well organised and funded by manufacturers.
- It had strong leadership – Richard Cobden, a calico manufacturer elected an MP in 1841, and John Bright, a Rochdale mill owner elected an MP in 1843, were both excellent speakers.
- Excellent use of communications was made with leaflets distributed in the penny post, and by lectures, public meetings and newspapers.
- Fund-raising bazaars – selling mugs, scarves, handkerchiefs with Anti-Corn Law slogans – promoted the cause.

What was the effect of the Irish Potato Famine?

In 1845 over half of the Irish potato crop was destroyed by potato blight. Potatoes formed the basic diet of the majority of Ireland's 8 million people, and they faced starvation. The situation was made worse by a poor harvest in England which meant that no corn could be sent to Ireland. There was an urgent need for imported grain.

Sir Robert Peel was the Conservative Prime Minister. He had spoken against the Corn Laws in 1815 and he listened to Cobden and Bright's arguments for repeal in Parliament. His father had been a cotton manufacturer, so he understood their reasoning. He became convinced that the repeal of the Corn Laws would benefit Britain. He also knew, however, that repeal was fiercely resisted by the landowners and farmers who made up most of the Conservative Party. These landowners felt threatened as they did not think that they would be able to compete against foreign corn if duties were removed.

Peel was in a very difficult position, but the potato famine meant he had to put forward the repeal, otherwise more people would starve. He failed to persuade his Cabinet of the need to repeal the Corn Laws and resigned in December 1845. Within 15 days he was returned as Prime Minister and after six months of fierce debating the Corn Laws were repealed on 24 June 1846.

Results of the repeal of the Corn Laws

- A major triumph for the ACLL.
- Farmers and landowners felt betrayed by Peel.
- Peel's political career was ruined – he resigned in July 1846.
- Farmers were not ruined and farming entered a very prosperous era.

◀ **SOURCE 7**
Cartoon showing the items sold at the ACLL bazaar.

Questions

1. Explain the meaning of free trade.

2. Why did Parliament introduce the Corn Laws in 1815?

3. What is the main argument against the Corn Laws put forward by Cobden in Source 5? Give two other reasons why manufacturers and industrialists wanted the repeal of the Corn Laws.

4. What can you learn from Source 6 about the Anti-Corn Law League?

5. With reference to each of the following statements, explain which was the most important reason for the repeal of the Corn Laws in 1846:
   (a) protests by the poor;
   (b) the Irish Potato Famine;
   (c) poor harvests;
   (d) the work of the Anti-Corn Law League.

2.3 *Why did farming prosper between 1850 and 1870* ?

Many farmers had expected economic ruin after the repeal of the Corn Laws, and between 1846 and 1849 imports of foreign corn doubled and prices did fall. However, by 1850, a new period of prosperity had begun for farmers. In fact 1850 to 1870 was such a successful time for farmers that it became known as **'The Golden Age of Agriculture'** or the period of 'High Farming'. Farming was profitable. Both tenant farmers and landowners were encouraged to invest more capital in the farms. Source 8 illustrates several reasons for the 'The Golden Age of Agriculture'.

> ## KEY IDEAS
>
> - Farmers did not suffer as a result of the repeal of the Corn Laws
> - Railways could transport fresh produce to towns
> - Artificial fertilisers increased the yield of the land
> - Drainage was improved
> - Steam-powered machinery was gradually introduced

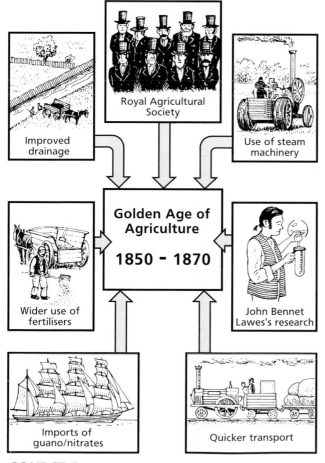

SOURCE 8 ▲
Reasons for the Golden Age of Agriculture.

Lack of overseas competition

The expected flood of foreign corn into Britain after the repeal of the Corn Laws did not arrive. Foreign competition was not as strong as farmers had feared, mainly because many corn-producing countries were engaged in wars. For example, **Russia** was fighting the Crimean War (1853-56), **Germany** was at war with Denmark (1863), Austria (1866) and France (1870-1871), and **America** was fighting its Civil War (1861-1865). These wars interrupted corn supplies to Britain.

The growth of population and increased urbanisation

By 1851 the population was 17.9 million and was still growing rapidly. The 1851 census showed that half the population now lived in towns – more people than ever before. Townspeople were relatively prosperous and had money to spend on food. Farmers realised that they had an expanding market for their meat and dairy products. This encouraged them to increase production to make more profit.

33

The expansion of railways

By 1850, over 6,000 miles of railways were in operation, and this had increased to 13,500 miles by 1870. Railways stimulated agriculture because perishable products such as milk, meat and vegetables could reach the growing industrial towns quickly. They also provided farmers with an easier way of getting livestock to market (Source 9). Animals arrived in better condition than when herds were driven along the roads, so they sold for a higher price. The trains also provided a more efficient way of transporting agricultural supplies such as seeds, fertilisers and farming implements.

The Royal Agricultural Society

The Society was founded in 1838 to promote interest in farming. It organised shows where farmers could see demonstrations of the new methods and latest machinery. It encouraged competition by arranging rewards for new discoveries, and published a journal giving details of the latest agricultural research.

Application of science to farming

In order to grow good quality crops, the soil needed to be well fertilised. Farmers had begun to add a variety of things to the soil including animal manure, soot and bones, but there was a need for artificial fertilisers. In the 1830s fertilisers had been imported from abroad including guano (bird droppings) from Peru and nitrates from Chile. John Bennet Lawes had begun experiments on his estate at Rothamsted, Hertfordshire in 1834, and established an experimental station there in 1843. He conducted experiments on all aspects of farming, types of seed, livestock breeding and crop rotations. He was particularly interested in the development of artificial fertilisers, and in 1843 he set up a factory at Deptford for producing super-phosphates. The use of artificial fertilisers greatly improved the quality of the soil and increased the yield of the crops.

Drainage improvements

Drainage had always been a problem for farmers. Water-logged soil was unsuitable for growing crops. In 1823 James Smith, a Scottish farmer, had successfully used shallow drains made by digging parallel trenches and lining the bottom with pebbles. By 1843, cylindrical clay pipes were introduced to

SOURCE 10 ▲
Institute of Research in Agriculture, Rothamsted, in 1890.

SOURCE 11 ▲
A steam-engine and threshing machine.

provide a cheap method of drainage. By 1850, the Government was giving cheap loans to farmers, repayable by instalments, to encourage them to lay drainage pipes. The results of improved drainage meant that farmers could now drain and plough heavy wet soil, which they had previously not been able to cultivate.

Steam-powered machines

Reaping machines were slowly being introduced. In 1826 Patrick Bell patented a reaping machine, but it was clumsy and needed horses to move it. The American, Cyrus McCormick, made a more practical reaper which was on display at the Great Exhibition in 1851. These mechanical reapers saved time and reduced labour costs. By 1870 there were 40,000 in use. Gradually steam threshing machines were introduced to thresh the cut corn. A common farming practice was steam ploughing, and cultivating by windlass – an engine was put at one end of a field, and a windlass at the other. The plough was pulled back and forth between the two.

Despite the advances in machinery, many farmers were still reluctant to use the new machines which were expensive and often broke down. Some farmers were still of the opinion '*hand work is best work*'. The machines for ploughing and reaping which were designed for American fields were still not really effective because British fields were too small to make use of them.

Questions

1. Read Source 9. What can you learn from this source about the transporting of animals by rail?

2. What favourable circumstances, beyond the farmers' control, had helped the years 1850 to 1870 to become known as 'The Golden Age of Agriculture'.

3. How successful were the new steam-powered machines?

4. You are a successful farmer living in the south of England in 1860. Write a letter to a friend in Manchester explaining the reasons why agriculture did not suffer after the repeal of the Corn Laws.

2.4 Why did some types of farming suffer a depression between 1870 and 1900 ?

The Golden Age of Agriculture came to an end in the 1870s, and farming experienced a bad depression. The worst periods were 1874-1884, and 1890-1896. The depression had many causes:

● **Wet summers:** Several cold, wet summers between 1873 and 1879 ruined crops and led to poor grain harvests.

● **Animal disease:** During the wettest summer on record in 1879, millions of sheep were destroyed because of foot rot and liver fluke. In 1883 foot and mouth disease infected cattle herds.

● **Increased foreign competition:** This was the major reason for the depression in farming.

Foreign competition

● **Corn:** By 1870 huge quantities of cheap corn were being imported into Britain, especially from America. America grew corn on the Prairies where it was very easy to use machinery, which made it cheaper. In 1874

80% of American corn was harvested by machine compared with only 47% in Britain. The steamship to England was also becoming cheaper as freight charges dropped. For example, in 1868 it cost 65s (£3.25) to send a ton of corn from Chicago to Liverpool, but in 1882 it only cost 24s (£2.20).

British corn farmers could not compete with the price of imported, cheaply grown corn. In 1873 imports of corn exceeded home production for the first time.

● **Wool** from Australia and New Zealand was cheaper than English wool.

● **Beef and Mutton.** In 1882 the first cargoes of refrigerated meat arrived from New Zealand (Source 13). The introduction of canning also made it possible for meat like corned beef from Argentina to be imported.

KEY IDEAS

● British farmers could not compete with cheap foreign imports

● Bad weather resulted in poor harvests

● Animal diseases were common

● Farmers changed from growing crops to rearing animals

● Market gardening developed

● Agricultural labourers left the land to work in towns

SOURCE 12

Essex ... Between 1880 and 1884 the number of farms given up either in despair, or for reasons over which the occupiers had no control, was stated to have been enormous ... On poor estates no attempt was made to bring the land round; it was left alone, and gradually 'tumbled down' to such coarse and inferior herbage as nature produced ... rents were reduced ... Only those who kept a considerable head of stock ... still continue in occupation.

The Royal Commission on Agriculture's 1897 report showed how arable farming in the south-east suffered most during the depression.

What were the effects of the agricultural depression?

The most severe effects were felt in the traditional corn-producing areas of the south and south-east of England as can be seen in Source 12.

Some farmers living near large towns became **market gardeners**. They grew fruit and vegetables to sell to people in towns who had a better standard of living and demanded a more varied diet.

Many farmers changed from arable (crop-growing) farming to **pastoral farming** (rearing animals) where the effects of foreign competition were less severe. Pastoral farmers were able to produce beef and mutton of much better quality than the imported refrigerated meat. People preferred fresh meat to canned or frozen. Milk, butter and cheese still had a market as well.

Pastoral farming needed fewer labourers than arable farming, and between 1870 and 1900 the number of farm labourers fell by 300,000. Many labourers moved to find work in the mines and factories where they could earn high wages, and others emigrated.

By the 1880s landowners had to accept lower rents from farm tenants, and lower profits. Some farmers went bankrupt. If tenant farmers left the land, landowners often could not find replacements, so a large number of farms were left empty. In general, land values fell and farming ceased to be a good investment.

What action did the Government take?

The Government were slow to act because by the 1880s fewer MPs were large landowners. Many town dwellers and working people had the vote, and they cared more about having cheap food than about the British farmers. However, the Government did take some action which included setting up Royal Commissions in 1879 and 1894 to investigate the causes of depression.

In spite of this action, British farming was still in a depressed condition in 1900, and agriculture was no longer the key occupation it had been a hundred years before.

Questions

1. Read Source 12.
   (a) Give two reasons why farmers might have given up their farms between 1870 and 1900.
   (b) Describe the condition of some of the poor estates in Essex.

2. Draw a diagram to show the causes of the depression in farming from 1870-1900.

3. How were the following affected by the depression in farming:
   arable (corn growing) farmers;
   landowners;
   townspeople;
   farm labourers?

◀ **SOURCE 13**
Frozen meat imported from New Zealand is unloaded in England.

3 THE TEXTILE REVOLUTION

3.1 *What were the advantages and disadvantages of the Domestic System*

Cloth production

In the early 18th century, woollen-cloth production was a source of great prosperity in Britain. Production took place in three main areas – East Anglia, the West Country and the West Riding of Yorkshire.

In East Anglia and the West Country, rich merchants (**merchant clothiers**) who had enough money (capital) bought wool from farmers. They rented looms and spinning wheels to cottage workers and 'gave-out' wool to them to make into cloth. Workers were paid on a '**piece-rate**', so their earnings depended on how much cloth they produced.

In the West Riding of Yorkshire, better-off farmer-weavers employed spinners to produce yarn for weaving. The West Riding became the most important wool-producing area during the 18th century. It had coal for heating water to wash the wool, a big labour force, transport and plenty of water power.

SOURCE 1 ▲
Workers spinning thread – you can see brushes used for carding on the floor.

What was the Domestic System?

Thousands of part-time workers produced cloth in their own homes, fitting this in with farm work.

Different family members were involved in the various stages of production.

- Children carded (untangled) the wool.
- Women spun the wool into yarn.
- Men wove the yarn into cloth on a loom, using a shuttle.
- The cloth was beaten, cleaned and made thicker by scrubbing it with Fuller's earth (a chemical) in a water mill.
- The cloth was stretched over large frames ('tenter-frames') and then dyed and bleached.
- Croppers used large shears to smooth the surface of the cloth. They often worked in small workshops. Their skill could increase the value of a roll of cloth by up to one-third.

What was good about the Domestic System?

- Families could work together, at their own pace and at home.
- Families had earnings from cloth manufacturing to live on if there was little farm work.
- When the wool trade was slack, workers had a plot of land to live off.

In 1724 Daniel Defoe found everyone in Halifax so busy that *'there was not a beggar nor an idle person to be seen ... all can gain their bread, even from the youngest to the most ancient'*.

What was bad about the Domestic System?

- The quality of cloth varied from one cottage to another.
- Merchant clothiers could exploit workers by underpaying them, or overcharging for the rent of spinning wheels and looms.
- Time was wasted 'giving out' the wool to the cottagers.
- Piece-rates were often very low.
- Cottages were often dusty, dirty and badly lit and ventilated.
- Production was slow. It was difficult to see how the Domestic System could meet the needs of the increasing population.

The woollen industry was very slow to introduce new technology. It was not until the 1870s that all woollen cloth was produced in factories by machinery. However, not all textile industries were slow to change. The cotton industry took the lead in Britain's **Industrial Revolution**.

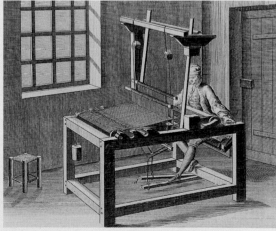

SOURCE 2 ▲
A handloom weaver, using the light from the upstairs window of his cottage.

39

3.2 *How did new technology affect the textile industry* **?**

What changes were taking place during the early 18th century?

Cotton was becoming more popular than wool. Demand was, of course, rising because of the increase in the population. But its popularity was due to cotton clothes being a sign of prosperity. Fashionable ladies said, '*Why have wool when you can have cotton?*' Cotton was more attractive, it was brighter and often patterned. It was also easier to wash. Although there had been problems with supplies of cotton from America, this situation improved after 1793 with the invention, by Eli Whitney, of a cotton gin. This speeded up the cleaning of the raw cotton at the plantation and brought costs down.

> ### KEY IDEAS
>
> - Cotton was becoming more popular than wool
> - Factory production was being introduced
> - New machines were speeding up spinning and weaving
> - Arkwright's Water Frame needed a new source of power
> - Hand spinners and weavers were ruined

Factory methods were introduced. Between 1718 and 1722, John and Thomas Lombe set up the first silk factory near Derby. The power source for the machines was a water wheel. Silk production was itself not important in Britain at this time. What was important, was that the Lombes showed how large-scale production could work in a country which was only used to small-scale cottage production. Their factory soon provided work for 1,500 people, and produced massive profits. The idea of factory production eventually spread.

Technology was improving for spinning and weaving.

◀**SOURCE 3**
Sir Richard Arkwright and a model of his spinning frame.

How did technology change spinning?

James Hargreaves and the Spinning Jenny, 1764: James Hargreaves (1720-79) invented a faster spinning machine. He had claimed his Spinning Jenny ('jenny' was short for 'engine') could spin 8 spindles at once. In 1770 a version which spun 16 spindles was patented (which meant that anyone who copied his ideas had to pay a royalty). The spindles were turned by one large hand-operated wheel.

His machines could produce so much thread that the price dropped dramatically. The weavers were pleased with his invention which supplied plenty of cheap thread for them to work with. However, hand spinners had to work much harder and produce more thread to make a living. He became so unpopular with hand spinners, that they smashed his machines and burned his house in Blackburn, Lancashire. Hargreaves left Blackburn and set up a factory in Nottingham.

The Spinning Jenny did have drawbacks. It needed a skilled operator. It produced a fine but weak thread – only suitable for the cross threads (the weft). There was still a need for further developments in spinning technology.

◀ SOURCE 4
The water wheel which drove the machinery in Arkwright's first water-powered mill.

Richard Arkwright and the Water Frame, 1769: Richard Arkwright (1732-92) was a barber and wig maker from Preston in Lancashire. He knew that there was a fortune to be made by anyone who could invent a workable spinning machine. He persuaded a clockmaker, John Kay, to help him build a spinning machine called a Frame. This early Frame used horse power. It had sets of rollers, each set going at a different speed. When the thread passed between them it was stretched; when it was wound on to a spindle, it was twisted, making it stronger. The thread was, however, rather coarse.

SOURCE 5
Arkwright's second mill (the first was destroyed by fire). ▲

Arkwright saw the possibilities of making huge profits from the spinning machine. He did not want one or two Frames in cottages. Instead, he wanted large numbers of machines under one roof. However, it took a huge amount of money to open a large scale enterprise. So Arkwright found a man with capital who was willing to invest in the business. This was Jedediah Strutt, a wealthy stocking manufacturer from Nottingham. Arkwright also found a skilled craftsman, Thomas Highs, who could build the Spinning Frames.

Strutt and Arkwright knew about the Lombes' silk factory. They decided to copy the idea and built their own spinning factory (called a 'mill'), at Cromford in Derbyshire. It was a good site as there was a plentiful water supply to provide the power for the mill. This was far better than the horses which Arkwright had used to power his early machines. Many frames could be worked off the power of a single water wheel.

Cromford Mill was opened in 1771. By 1782, Arkwright was employing 5,000 workers. Visitors were impressed by the size of the mill, and by Arkwright's success.

SOURCE 7

Richard Guest, a historian, wrote this in 1823:

By borrowing from Thomas High's inventions, Arkwright lived to gain a princely fortune. Meanwhile the man who had invented these ingenious machines died in poverty.

Arkwright built a village for his workers, and a school for their children. His business was so successful he built other mills in Nottingham, Derby and Lancashire. But had Arkwright stolen the idea for the Frame? A machine invented in 1738 by Lewis Paul and a carpenter, John Wyatt, also had sets of rollers to spin the thread. In 1784 Arkwright was accused of 'stealing' the ideas for his invention, and he was taken to court. He lost the case, and so lost his patent. However, Arkwright's reputation and fortune had been made. He was knighted in 1786, becoming Sir Richard Arkwright. When he died in 1792 he was having a fine house, Willesley Castle, built for himself.

Arkwright completely changed the way industry was organised. He brought people, power, cotton and money together to create large-scale production and one of the first '**factories**' ever built. The small-scale cottage system which had existed for so long was now doomed.

SOURCE 8

In 1775, Arkwright claimed that he:

had perfected Certain Machines which would be of use to the public for Spinning and built on Principles very different from any other that had ever been built.

Samuel Crompton and the Spinning Mule, 1779: Machine spinning was providing weavers with thread which was either fine but too weak – from the Jenny – or strong but coarse – from the Water Frame. Samuel Crompton (1753-1827), a weaver from Bolton in Lancashire, crossed the designs of a Jenny and a Water Frame to make a single machine. He called it a 'Mule' (because a mule is a cross between a horse and a donkey).

This machine produced a fine, strong thread. From the start, the Mules were large machines, spinning 300-400 threads at once, so were designed to be used in factories. By 1825, even larger Mules were

SOURCE 9

From Ned Ludd, to a Huddersfield mill owner in 1812.

Sir,
Information has been given in, that you are the holder of those detestable Shearing Frames ... if they are not taken down by the end of the week I shall detach 200 men to destroy them, burning your buildings to ashes.

in production. One, developed by Richard Roberts, could spin 2,000 threads at once.

Not surprisingly, the Mule was widely used by factory owners. By 1860, 400,000 were in use. Unfortunately, Crompton had not taken out a patent on his machine so he earned very little from the success of his design. However, Parliament did make him a grant of £5,000.

The Luddites: what happened to those who opposed the changes in the textile industry?

Violent protests against the new machines were made by gangs of machine breakers called Luddites. They took their name from their 'leader', Ned Ludd, (Source 9) although there is no evidence he was a real person. Desperate men, very often skilled weavers or croppers (the men who finished the surface of the cloth by hand), attacked factories and broke up the machines that were ruining their livelihood. Trouble broke out in 1811, and then recurred at several times in the 1820s and 1830s.

Some people saw Luddites as proud men whose traditional skills were under threat. However, other people thought that protest was wrong because nothing could stop the introduction of machines. They thought that progress was good because an entire family could earn wages in factories. The authorities were so concerned that soldiers were used to round up the ringleaders, who were then either hanged or transported to Australia.

Questions

1. How did the Domestic System work?

2. What were the advantages and disadvantages of the Domestic System of textile production?

3. Here are some reasons why the Domestic System was in decline during the 18th century:
   - the population was rising
   - the use of new spinning machines
   - the problems of the Domestic System.

   (a) Which was the most important reason for the decline of the Domestic System? Why?

   (b) What other factors played a part in the decline of the Domestic System?

4. Sir Richard Arkwright was:
   (a) a clever businessman;
   (b) someone who just pirated other people's ideas;
   (c) the 'father of the factory system'.

   Using the text and Sources 6, 7 and 8 explain which reputation Arkwright really deserves.

5. How might a Luddite defend his actions against factory owners?

6. Explain why Source 10 is a biased piece of evidence about the Luddites.

SOURCE 10
This, is how one artist portrayed Luddite action in 1811. ▶

How did technology change weaving?

Kay's Flying Shuttle: In 1733, John Kay (1704-80), a weaver and clockmaker from Lancashire, developed the Flying Shuttle. It was a clever way of speeding up weaving. The weaver pulled a string and a shuttle 'flew' across the cloth, so the weft threads were put in position quickly. Cloth could be wider as the shuttle did not have to be passed across by hand.

The weavers hated it because the new shuttle meant that only one man, not two, was needed to make 'broadcloth'. Some weavers were put out of work. Because the Flying Shuttle speeded up weaving, weavers used thread faster than it could be spun. Thread went up in price.

Weavers were angry, and they burned down Kay's house in Bury, Lancashire. Kay fled to France.

Opposition from weavers also meant that the Flying Shuttle was not in widespread use until 1760. After 1760 the challenge was to invent a machine which could spin thread more quickly, to keep the weavers supplied (see pages 41-42).

SOURCE 11

In The Origin of the New System of Manufacture, *published in 1828, W. Radcliffe, wrote about the period from 1788 to 1803 when there was thread from the Mules and much demand for cloth:*

Weavers' dwellings and small gardens were clean and neat – all the family well clad – the men with each a watch in his pocket, and the women dressed to their own fancy ... every house well furnished with a clock, handsome tea services ... and ornaments ... many cottage families had their cow.

SOURCE 12

A Parliamentary investigation in 1827 found that because of competition from machines:

There is little hope that any revival of trade can bring back the employment of distressed handloom weavers ... the sum of £75,000 will be enough to remove, provision and locate 1,200 families in North America.

Edmund Cartwright's Power Loom, 1785 – the rise and fall of handloom weaving: Although hand spinning as a trade was dying out, the number of hand weavers grew from 75,000 in 1795 to 250,000 in 1833. There was plenty of thread to use from Water Frames and Mules but not enough weavers to use it. As a result weavers could earn high wages (probably twice the average skilled wage) and, as Source 11 shows, they were keen to show how well off they were.

The first attempt at a power loom, made by the Reverend Edmund Cartwright (1743-1828) in 1785, failed to work very well. As it was made of wood, it was always breaking down. Yet again the invention of new technology had no immediate effect on the industry. In 1803, Horrocks of Stockport made the important step forward of building a metal loom, but this was clumsy.

It was another twenty years before reliable power looms were made, and the numbers in use started to increase. By 1850 there were 250,000 of them being used in factories. The machines could weave nine times faster than hand weavers. The weavers could not compete with the machines. Wages fell and they had to choose between facing desperate poverty, or going to work in factories.

SOURCE 13
Mr Hacking was one of the last handloom weavers. He is pictured here in 1890.▼

Questions

1. Make up a table of textile inventions using these headings:
   Name of inventor;
   Date;
   Name of machine;
   What problem did it solve;
   Drawbacks.

2. 'The introduction of new machines did not mean that immediate changes took place in industry.' Do you agree? Explain your answer.

3. Explain how the handloom weavers were affected by the development of textile machinery.

   Mention how prosperous they were at first, and how they later suffered a decline.

4. How useful are Sources 11 and 12 to a historian studying the handloom weavers?

SOURCE 14
For making 24 yards of cloth which would take a week, a Bolton handloom weaver was paid:

1795	34s	(£1.70)
1805	25s	(£1.25)
1820	10s	(50p)
1829	5s 6d	(27 $\frac{1}{2}$p)

3.3 What changes had taken place in the textile industry by the middle of the 19th century?

Where was the industry concentrated?

As steam-powered machines began to be used, textile production moved to those fast-growing towns which were near to coal, the labour supply, and to the markets which would buy their products. Two areas developed particularly quickly.

Lancashire was becoming the heart of cotton making.

- Cotton imports from Turkey, India and Egypt could easily reach Lancashire through the port of Liverpool.
- There were plenty of workers, some with experience of spinning and weaving.
- The climate was damp, which helped to stop the threads from breaking. The fast flowing Pennine streams provided power for the water wheels and soft water, ideal for washing, bleaching and dyeing the cotton.
- Places such as Manchester had banks able to loan capital. There were good transport

SOURCE 15 ▲
A water-powered mill from the early 18th century.

links, as well as nearby coal to power the steam engines, and to heat the water which washed and bleached the cotton.

Glasgow and **Clydeside** (the area round the river Clyde) also became an important cotton making area, famous for its Paisley designs.

SOURCE 16

A cotton-spinning establishment offers a remarkable example of how, by the use of the very great power, an enormous quantity of the easiest work can be accomplished. Often we may see in a single building a 100 horse-power steam-engine, which has the strength of 880 men, set in motion 50,000 spindles. The whole requires the service of but 750 workers. But these machines, with the assistance of that mighty power can produce as much yarn as formerly could hardly have been spun by 200,000 men, so that each man can now produce as much as formerly required 166! In 12 hours the factory produces a thread 62,000 miles in length, that is to say which would encircle the whole earth $2^1/_2$ times!

Edward Baines, History of the Cotton Manufacture in Great Britain, *1835.*

How had the textile industry changed?

By 1850, cotton cloth accounted for 50% of the value of Britain's export trade. This was a spectacular growth in the importance of cotton – it was by then called 'King Cotton'. Handloom weaving was dying out, and steam-driven machinery had been quickly introduced.

Wool, on the other hand, did less well. People preferred to wear cotton.

Woollen manufacturers had been slow to introduce machinery. The wool industry lagged about 20 years behind the cotton industry in becoming fully mechanised. Wool did continue to dominate industry in the West Riding of Yorkshire. It had coal, transport and a work force as well as water for washing the wool. Despite shortages of raw wool the industry had survived, using imported raw wool from Australia and New Zealand.

◀ **SOURCE 17**
A huge flax mill, built in the 1840s in Leeds.

Questions

1. Imagine you are a 19th-century factory owner. What reasons would you give to a banker for wanting money to move your factory to a Lancashire town?

2. Why had cotton become more important than wool by 1850?

3. How useful are Sources 15 and 17 in showing the changes in the textile industry between 1700 and 1850? Explain your answer.

4. Explain Baines' attitude to the 'textile revolution' in Source 16.

4 IRON & STEEL

4.1 What problems faced the iron industry in 1700?

THIS SECTION ANSWERS:

4.1 What problems faced the iron industry in 1700?

4.2 Which were the most important changes in iron making during the 18th century?

4.3 What were the important changes in iron and steel during the 19th century?

At the beginning of the 18th century there was an iron shortage. Old nails had to be saved, straightened by blacksmiths, and re-used. Half Britain's iron was imported, mainly from Sweden and Russia.

During the century the need for iron increased to meet demand from:

- **Warfare** – for guns, cannons, wheel axles, nails, anchors.
- **Industry** – for textile machinery, coal mining winding gear, waggons, rails, steam pumps and engines, iron girders and pillars for mills and workshops.
- **Agriculture** – for new machines, such as the Rotherham Plough.
- Increasing **population** – for domestic items such as pots, pans, bedsteads, locks and bolts, and household tools.
- **Trade and transport** – for making barges, bridges and ships.

To produce iron, iron ore has to be heated to a high temperature in a furnace so that molten iron runs out. (Source 2 shows the stages of iron making.) The fuel used in 1700 was charcoal (partly burned wood). The early British iron industry was located in wooded areas,

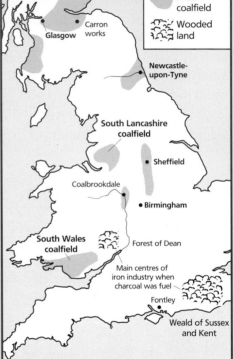

SOURCE 1 ▲
Map of the changing location of iron making.

48

such as the Forest of Dean, where there was iron ore, water and timber to make charcoal (see Source 1). However, there was a shortage of timber, which was also used for shipbuilding, house construction, brewing, building, farming tools and furniture construction. This was a problem because it took about 100 tons to make about 25 tons of charcoal. Charcoal burning was also a slow process.

Coal was plentiful and cheap, but could not be used as its sulphur content would ruin the iron, making it too brittle. Without another fuel, the British iron industry seemed doomed.

The iron that was produced, **Pig iron**, had its drawbacks. If melted in a furnace, it could be cast into large, solid objects such as pipes, cannon, and large pots. This was **cast iron**. Because it contained a lot of carbon, cast iron cracked if it was hammered into a shape. So, some pig iron was converted into **wrought iron** by heating it in a forge until red hot and soft. It was then hammered to get rid of impurities. Hammering took place in small workshops. It was a slow process which meant that wrought iron was expensive. Wrought iron could be shaped into rails, machine parts, springs, tools or sent to a slitting mill to be made into strips for nail manufacture.

Transporting the iron was difficult. Moving bulky goods by pack horse, using muddy roads or dirt tracks full of pot holes, was not only very slow but also expensive. It was not until canals were built and roads developed after the 1760s that things improved.

KEY IDEAS

- There was a lot of demand for iron

Problems for the iron industry included:

- scattered location of iron making sites
- shortage of timber for charcoal
- slow and expensive transport
- shortage of good quality wrought iron

SOURCE 2
The stages of iron making.

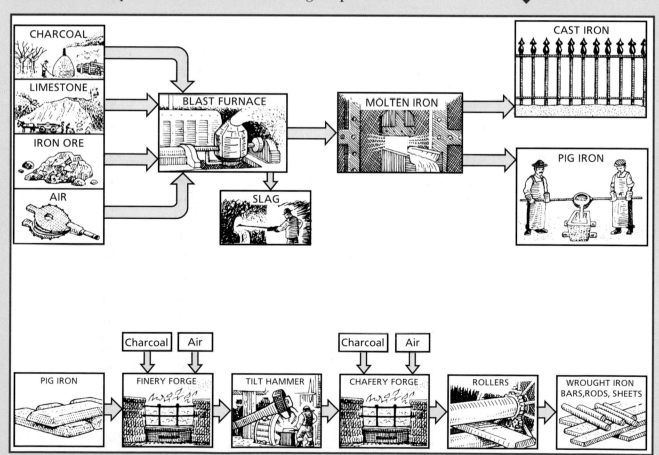

4.2 Which were the most important changes in iron making during the 18th century ?

The Darbys of Coalbrookdale

In 1708, Abraham Darby I rented a disused furnace in Coalbrookdale, Shropshire, and began experimenting with a different type of fuel to smelt the iron ore – it was coke (partly-burned coal). His father was a nailer, and he had learned his trade in iron foundries before moving to the Birmingham malt industry, where coke was already being used as a fuel to dry the malt used for brewing beer.

Coalbrookdale was a good site for iron production. It had:

● water for power, and the River Severn for transport;

● local outcrops of iron ore and coal, as well as charcoal for the forges; and

● a demand for the iron was nearby – in Staffordshire and Birmingham.

Luckily, Darby was able to use local 'clod' coal, which was very low in sulphur content, to turn into coke.

In 1709, Darby succeeded in using coke to smelt iron ore. Coke contains little sulphur, and produces higher temperatures in the furnace. As a result, bigger furnaces could be

built, lowering costs, and more iron could be smelted.

> ## KEY IDEAS
>
> ● First use of coke as a fuel in iron smelting 1709
>
> ● World's first iron bridge built 1779
>
> ● Cast iron production increased, but wrought iron was still in short supply
>
> ● Henry Cort developed the puddling furnace to make more wrought iron

How important was Abraham Darby I?

An important step forward had been taken, although Darby's work was not immediately adopted by other ironmasters. In 1750 there were still only three coke furnaces, compared to 71 charcoal furnaces. Only in 1790 did the number of coke furnaces outnumber the charcoal ones. Why did this change happen so slowly?

SOURCE 3 ▼
A timeline for the development of Coalbrookdale.

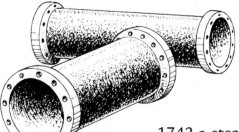

1722 cast iron cylinders made

1742 a steam engine pumped water back to the pool so that the bellows could still work the furnace during the dry summer months

1748 wooden rails laid – 1 waggon could carry the coal carried by 12 packhorses

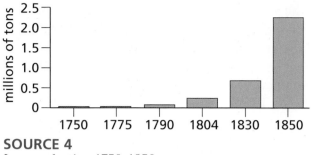

SOURCE 4
Iron production 1750–1850. ▲

Now that furnaces were beginning to use coke, it made sense for iron making to move away from wooded areas to the coalfields of Staffordshire, South Yorkshire and South Wales. However, this change of location only began to take place slowly after the 1850s. Why? Steam pumping was not yet fully developed, so furnaces still had to be close to water power to work the bellows and create the air blast.

Abraham Darby has been accused of refusing to share what he had discovered. This is not true. Darby made agreements with other iron makers to build furnaces. They must have shared the information about the coke process. What is more likely, is that prices affected how fast coke was adopted. It was not until the 1760s that it became much cheaper to use coke instead of charcoal. Until then most iron masters were not prepared to invest in new furnaces.

Darby's new process could only produce cast and pig iron. It had then to be taken to the forge for hammering into wrought iron. This slowed production down.

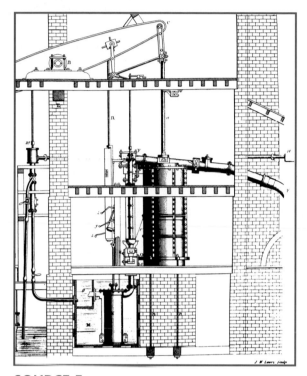

SOURCE 5
Coalbrookdale produced cylinders for Boulton and Watt's steam engines.

Abraham Darby I died in 1717, aged 39. He had founded a family business that would become very profitable during the 18th century under the direction of its managers Richard Ford, Richard Reynolds, Abraham Darby II and Abraham Darby III.

The expansion of the iron industry

Other ironworks began to open on Clydeside and in South Wales. By 1830 there were about 300 furnaces in Britain – nearly 200 of them in South Wales. The expansion took place after the start of the French Wars in 1793 (Source 4).

1749-66 experiments to make wrought iron in a furnace

1767 iron rails laid to link furnaces, river and coal mines

1776 a steam engine provided the air blast to the furnace

1779 Abraham Darby III built the world's first iron bridge

Henry Cort – the 'puddling and rolling' process

Cast iron was plentiful, but it still took hours to hammer it into wrought iron. Henry Cort was a naval contractor who knew that the Royal Navy was desperately short of wrought iron. He looked at experiments by the Wood brothers and Peter Onions to find a solution to the shortage. The Wood brothers had developed the 'Staffordshire process'. This produced a little wrought iron by smelting it in pots so it did not mix with the coal in the furnace and pick up any impurities. Peter Onions had tried a process called 'puddling'.

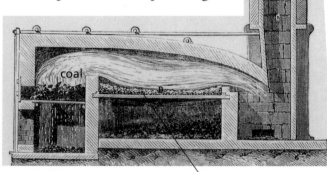

coal

molten pig iron being turned into wrought iron

SOURCE 6
Cort's reverberatory furnace. ▲

In 1783 Cort patented his own puddling furnace. He used coal, keeping it separate from the pig iron, and the heat reflected ('reverberated') off the roof of the furnace. The molten iron could then be puddled by a skilled worker – this involved stirring the liquid iron so that impurities would come to the surface and be burned off. It left purer, wrought iron in the furnace. When the iron was cooling and turning spongy, it was taken out in balls ('blooms') weighing up to 40 kilograms.

In 1784, Cort patented the second part of his process – rolling. The hot iron was passed between grooved rollers which shaped it into bars, strips, rails and plates. Bringing both puddling and rolling together was the real contribution made by Henry Cort.

Cort's process could produce 15 tons in 1 hour compared to 1 ton in 12 hours produced by hammering in a forge. It was quicker and, because the process used coal instead of coke, it was cheaper.

However, this method took a long time to come into general use. One problem was that it took 2 tons of pig iron to produce 1 ton of wrought iron in the furnace. Another problem was that Cort became bankrupt when his partner, Samuel Jellicoe, was convicted of fraud. (Fortunately Cort was granted a Government pension of £200 a year.)

The ironmaster who realised the advantages of Cort's process was **Richard Crawshay of Merthyr Tydfil**. He built rows of puddling furnaces on a larger scale than Cort. In 1784 his furnaces made 500 tons of iron a year – by 1809 this had risen to 10,000 tons. This mass-produced iron meant that prices fell.

● Ironmaking now moved near coalfields, where coal fuelled the furnaces as well as the steam engines. South Wales, Scotland (Clydeside), the Black Country to the north

SOURCE 8
Cort's rolling machinery. ▶

of the Birmingham area, and South Yorkshire became the major iron-making centres.

John 'Iron Mad' Wilkinson

This ruthless ironmaster increased the number of ways iron was used. By marrying into a family with money, Wilkinson expanded his father's iron foundry and built new ones in Shropshire and in France. His works were soon turning out products made from iron – the world's first iron barge in 1787, iron pipes to carry water round Paris, parts for the world's first iron bridge, and carefully bored-out cylinders for Boulton and Watt's steam engines (see page 66). Accurate technology was vital. If the cylinders were badly bored out, the pistons would not fit properly and steam pressure would be lost. Wilkinson's lathes, which were also used to bore out cannon, were a success. His close association with Boulton and Watt led Wilkinson to experiment with using steam engines – first to blow air into the furnace, and then to work the huge forge hammers which shaped the iron and made it purer.

His empire grew, as did his range of products. He even had an iron coffin made for himself, although the story goes that he was too fat to squeeze into it when he died in 1808.

◀ **SOURCE 7**
Cort's puddling technique.

Questions

1. Look at the following list of problems faced by the iron industry. How was each problem solved?

   (a) 1709 – a shortage of fuel to smelt the iron.

   (b) 1742 – a shortage of water to power the Coalbrookdale bellows.

   (c) 1767 – the need for better transport at Coalbrookdale.

   (d) 1783 – the shortage of wrought iron.

   (e) 1784 – the need for more iron bars, strips and rails.

2. Why was there so much more demand for iron in the 1700s?

3. Why was wrought iron so much more useful than cast iron? Why was it in short supply during the 1700s?

4. Why did the iron industry move location after the 1750s? Why did this happen so slowly?

5. Who was more important to the development of the iron industry in the 18th century: Abraham Darby I, Henry Cort or John Wilkinson? Explain your answer.

4.3 What were the important changes in iron and steel during the 19th century?

Why did iron making develop so rapidly in the 19th century?

Iron was the key to the Industrial Revolution. Steam engines and the development of 19th century transport, created a huge need for iron. Railways, bridges and Brunel's iron ships needed larger iron plates, bars and rails. Technology had to keep pace.

● The blast of air was vital to making sure that the furnace reached very high temperatures. James Neilson, in 1828, hit upon the idea that if the air blast was pre-heated, then fuel could be saved. Neilson showed that this simple solution could produce three times more iron while using the same amount of fuel.

● Realising that industry needed large pieces of iron, James Nasmyth, around 1839 and 1840, created his steam hammer (Source 10). Without this huge machine, Brunel could never have created large ships such as the *Great Eastern*.

> ### KEY IDEAS
> ● Demand for iron increased rapidly
> ● Steel was more flexible and stronger than iron
> ● Demand for steel overtook iron

SOURCE 9
A Bessemer Converter.
▼

SOURCE 10
Nasmyth's own painting of his steam hammer. ▲

Why did steel become so important?

Steel is a purer form of iron, containing only a little carbon. It is both more flexible and much stronger – extremely useful in the hands of shipbuilders, bridge builders, railway engineers and manufacturers of machinery.

The steel produced in the 1700s was expensive and in short supply. At the end of the 1740s, Benjamin Huntsman, a Doncaster clockmaker, developed a method of making steel in small clay pots called crucibles. First, the clay crucible was lined with ground glass and a little charcoal. Then iron that had undergone heating for over a week was placed in the crucible, and smelted at a very high

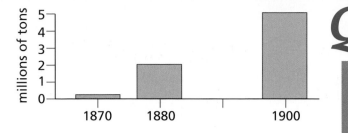

SOURCE 11
Steel production (Britain). ▲

temperature. The small amounts of steel produced were very good for Sheffield's cutlery and scythe-making industries, as well as for making springs for clocks. But more steel was needed. Source 12 shows the inventions and methods that eventually increased steel production.

Questions

1. What are the advantages of using steel?

2. What problems faced the steel industry in the 18th century?

3. Explain what is happening in the picture of the Bessemer Converter (Source 9).

4. Which was more important: the Bessemer Converter, the Open Hearth Process or the Basic Process? Why?

5. How could a British invention, the Basic Process, both help and hinder the British steel industry?

SOURCE 12 *The development of steel making.* ▼

	Inventor 1 Sir Henry Bessemer	Inventor 2 William Siemens	Inventor 3 Percy Gilchrist with his cousin Sidney Gilchrist-Thomas
Date	1856	1866	1879
The invention	The Bessemer Converter	The Open Hearth Process	The Basic Process
How it worked	A pear-shaped Converter was charged (filled) with pig iron. The Converter was then turned until upright – a blast of hot air was then blown through the Converter. This would create a shower of sparks and flames, as impurities were burned off. The Converter was then turned again so that the slag and then the steel could be poured out. (See Source 9).	Molten iron and scrap were placed in a hearth, and air – heated to very high temperatures by gas – was blown over the iron. The temperature inside the furnace could reach 1,650°C. The impurities were burned off.	Using limestone to line the converter meant that iron ore containing phosphorus could be used.
The product	'Mild steel', as it was called, was seven times cheaper to produce than before.	As less fuel was used the steel was cheaper.	Steel was made from British iron ores.
The drawback	It was impossible to use iron ore which contained phosphorus in the Converter. Unfortunately, most of Britain's ores were phosphoric.	As in the case of the Bessemer Converter, iron ore containing no phosphorus had to be imported from Spain and Sweden.	This invention also helped Britain's rivals, the USA and Germany, to develop their iron ores, which also contained phosphorus. Both countries overtook British steel production by 1914.

55

5 COAL

5.1 *What was the coal industry like in 1700?*

SOURCE 1
An adit mine. ▼

Coal seam - 1·5 metres thick

Water drained off

In 1700 only about 2 to 3 million tons of coal were produced a year. Mines were small, not very deep, and located in the countryside. It was not unusual for the miners to help with harvesting crops as well, especially when coal pits were on the estates of big landowners, such as Earl Fitzwilliam in South Yorkshire.

Most of Britain's coal came from the north-east – Durham and Northumberland. Coal was dug out from near the surface, and loaded on river boats called 'keels' and then on to sea-going 'collier' boats. (This coal was known as '**sea-coal**'). Most was taken to London, because the quickly-growing capital needed power. Transporting coal so far was, however, unusual. Moving it by pack-horse was slow and expensive, so coal from mines in other areas, such as Lancashire, South Wales, South Yorkshire and the Midlands, was used locally. Most coal was used in homes for heating, although it was also needed by brewers, soap boilers, sugar refiners, dyers, and manufacturers of bricks and salt.

Early miners never went very far beneath the surface. **1. Drift mines** just followed the coal seam into a hillside.

2. Miners in drift mines constantly battled against water which could not escape from the workings. An **adit mine** was a drift mine which gained its name from the drainage channel (adit) which was cut to allow the water to escape (Source 1).

3. In **bell pits** (Source 2), a ladder or hoist helped the miners reach the coal which then had to be hauled to the surface. If the 'bell' became too wide, there was a danger of a cave-in, so another bell-pit would be dug nearby.

KEY IDEAS

- Coal was mined near to the surface
- Production was small scale
- Demand for coal was increasing rapidly

SOURCE 2 ▲
A bell pit.

The industry remained small in scale. In South Yorkshire some mines only employed five men. However, during the 18th century all this changed. Coal mining became big business.

Why was there so much more demand for coal after 1700?

In the 18th century coal was used:
- to make iron, and in the growing tin, copper and lead industries;
- by Newcomen's steam engines and, later, by Boulton and Watt's engines;
- to fuel the steam engines in the textile mills of Lancashire and Yorkshire which were slowly turning to steam power;
- in homes in the rapidly growing towns.

Iron producers had faced many problems in finding the best fuel for their industry until about the 1780s when a new furnace allowed them to use coal (see page 52). By the end of the 18th century, the iron industry was using vast amounts of coal.

Even more coal was needed in the 19th century:
- It was exported to countries that had little coal.
- Railways and steamships developed which used enormous amounts of coal as fuel.
- It was the raw material for the gas industry. Gas was used for street lighting after the mid-19th century.

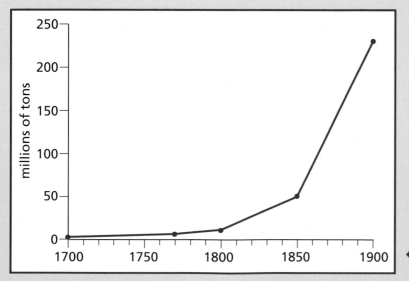

◀ **SOURCE 3**
Rise in coal production 1700-1900.

5.2 How far were the problems faced by miners solved by 1900 ?

Mines became deeper and deeper as more coal was needed. What problems and dangers did this cause?

Finding the coal seams: Miners relied on experience to find the seams. In the 1820s James Ryan invented a drill to bring samples of rock up from underground. The samples showed whether there was coal underneath the surface or not.

Extracting the coal: Throughout the 18th and 19th centuries miners relied on picks and shovels, not machines, to dig out the coal. In Lancashire and the Midlands, miners undercut the seam and drove in wedges at the top to bring the wall of coal crashing down. Despite the increasing use of pit props, the roof often collapsed at the same time. In parts of the north of England, the 'pillar and stall' (also called 'pillar and bord') method was used. Blocks of coal were dug out, leaving large pillars of coal to hold up the roof.

KEY IDEAS

Deeper mines increased the problems of:

- locating the coal seams
- extracting the coal and moving it underground
- poisonous and explosive gases, and flooding

Mine owners would not invest in cutting equipment, and Source 4 shows how productivity (the amount produced by each miner) actually fell. Even in 1913, 92% of all coal was dug out by pick and shovel. Coal was the only industry that failed to mechanise production. The technology that was introduced was mainly for bringing the coal to the surface or trying to improve safety.

Moving the coal: At the beginning of the 18th century, women and older children dragged baskets of coal (called 'corves') along narrow tunnels, to the bottom of the shafts, and then carried the baskets up steep ladders to get to the surface. From the 1760s, if the tunnels were high enough, pit ponies were used to pull waggons on wooden rails (later on iron rails). Horse-drawn hoists (whims or gins) could haul

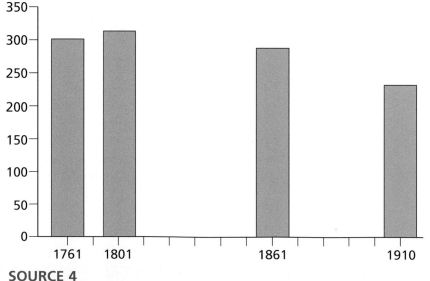

SOURCE 4
The number of tons of coal produced by each miner 1761-1910. ▲

58

SOURCE 5
An artist's impression of an explosion of firedamp. ▲

the coal up the shaft, but horses were expensive and slow, probably only hauling 100 tons a day. James Watt's steam engines could haul much more, but they were expensive to buy.

Improvements in transport very gradually made it easier to take the coal from the mines to where it was needed. Canals were an immediate success. The Duke of Bridgewater's canal, built in 1761, took coal to Manchester from Worsley, halving its cost (see pages 86-87). After 1767, horse-drawn waggons on iron rails ran from the pit to rivers or canals for loading onto keels. In the 19th century, steam locomotives allowed coal to be moved quickly and cheaply.

Flooding of mines: Water in the tunnels was a great danger to miners. Hand pumps or horse gins could not draw enough water out of the pits. In 1706, Thomas Newcomen, a blacksmith, invented a steam engine to draw water out of mines. It used enormous amounts of coal, was slow and did not work very efficiently. Despite this, 140 were in use by 1781. James Watt's engines worked more quickly and pumped out much more water and they slowly came into use after 1776. The drawback of all these early steam engines was that they were limited to making a beam rise and fall (see page 66). James Watt's development of the 'sun and planet' gear made it possible for a steam engine to turn a wheel. This engine could then pump water and lift coal to the surface. These engines were quickly in demand.

Gas was responsible for a very high death toll. One type of gas, 'chokedamp', suffocated those who breathed it in. Another type, methane or 'firedamp', exploded if it came into contact with candles or steel mills which produced showers of sparks (see Source 5). One way of trying to stop pockets of gas collecting was to dig extra ventilation shafts. As Source 6 shows, an iron basket containing burning coals was in one shaft. This caused a draught (because hot air rises), pulling 'bad' air out of the pit and fresh air down the other shaft. But in pits where there were large pockets of firedamp, the coals themselves could cause explosions. If owners of small pits did not want to spend money on sinking ventilation shafts, a 'fireman' dressed in soaking-wet sacking and holding a very long pole with a flame at its tip, was sent to ignite the gas at the coal face.

Around 1796, John Buddle, who was the manager of a pit in the north east of England, developed an exhaust air pump. It consisted of large fans which sucked gas out of one shaft and fresh air down another shaft to create a flow of air through the tunnels. Source 5 shows how trappers were needed to open and shut trap doors below ground to ensure that the air would flow through all the tunnels. Few owners introduced this technology, and miners continued to die. It was not until 1862 that all pits were required by law to have double ventilation shafts.

The Reverend John Hodgson, from Sunderland, set up the Society for the Prevention of Accidents in Mines in 1813. He wanted someone to design a type of light for miners that would be safe to use. This happened around 1815, when Sir Humphrey Davy designed the **Miners' Safety Lamp**. It had a flame which was surrounded by wire gauze. The gauze spread the heat over a wider area, stopping gas from making contact with the flame. If dangerous gases were present, the colour of the flame would change.

Despite some improvements that George Stephenson made to Davy's lamp, it was not an immediate success. As Source 8 states, workmen did not understand how to use the lamp. Some took the gauze off because the light was so poor. If it was left on, the gauze was not kept clean of coal dust. Owners mistakenly thought that the lamp kept miners safe, even if they went deeper underground

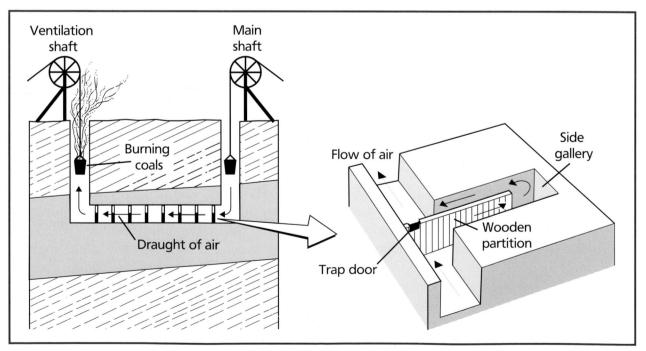

SOURCE 6
Mine ventilation. ▲

SOURCE 7

A mining accident at Barnsley in 1866 seen from the surface. ▲

SOURCE 8

Charles Martin, in the First Mine Inspector's Report, *1851 recorded:*

The idea behind this lamp is not thoroughly understood by the workmen and overlookers. Davy recommended a wire gauze containing no fewer than 784 openings in a square inch. He warned the miner not to expose it to a rapid current of inflammable air unless protected by a shield half encircling the gauze; he warned against it after the wire became 'red hot'.

Lamps are now made which contain 600 openings and shields are seldom seen. The gauze is seen at times red hot, and smeared outside with grease and coal dust.

The Davy lamp is disliked by the miner because of its feeble light. To obtain better light the gauze is sometimes taken off, endangering his own and fellow workmen's lives.

where there was even more gas. As a result, explosions continued, and so did huge loss of life (Source 7). The lighting problem continued until electric lamps were used underground in the 1890s.

Technology was not put to good use in coal mining. Instead human labour was exploited. There was a plentiful supply of workers who would accept any wages. Miners risked choking dust which settled on their lungs. They risked injuries from riding on the winding ropes or tubs which went up and down the shafts, because the ropes frayed or snapped. Wire cables were not used until the 1830s. Many people thought that mining families lived a savage and uncivilised life. They were the product of filthy, damp and squalid conditions underground. Until 1842, women worked alongside men underground, which many people thought was morally wrong. Investigations into working conditions in mines horrified the public (see page 73).

Questions

1. Why was coal mined on such a small scale at the beginning of the 18th century?

2. How far was flooding the worst problem that was faced in deep mines?

3. 'The needs of the iron industry were the main reason why coal production expanded rapidly at the end of the 18th century.' Do you agree with this statement? Explain your answer.

4. How far did the miners' safety lamp make the coal mines safer?

6 POWER FOR INDUSTRY

6.1 Did industry have a reliable source of power in the 18th century?

THIS SECTION ANSWERS:

6.1 Did industry have a reliable source of power in the 18th century?

6.2 How far did steam engine technology develop in the 18th century?

6.3 How important was the steam engine to the Industrial Revolution?

For much of the 18th century, there was no reliable source of industrial power. Until the 1780s, when more effective steam engines were built, industry had to rely on muscle power, horses (Source 1), wind and water. Of these, water power was the most important. Early textile mills were built next to fast flowing rivers so that the huge water wheels could turn the machinery inside. Water wheels could also grind corn, work bellows (to produce an air blast for furnaces) or power tilt hammers.

What were the problems with water power?

Water wheels were expensive to build. A dam to store the water to ensure a constant supply was an extra expense. There were different types of wheel (Source 2), and some types were better than others. John Smeaton showed in 1759 that undershot wheels, where the water hits the wheel at the bottom, were only 22% efficient in turning the water energy into power. The breast wheel and overshot wheels were far more powerful. Riverside sites were in the countryside where there were fewer workers available. An average of two weeks' work a year was lost because of difficulties keeping the water at the right level for the wheel, such as during drought in summer or ice in winter.

Industry continued to use water power, even when steam engines had been introduced. This was not surprising. The early steam engines did not work well and they failed to produce as much power as some of the largest wheels, such as Jedediah Strutt's which was 23 feet wide and produced 200 horse power. If steam engines were bought, they were used to improve water power. For example, the Darby family used a steam engine to pump water into a pond which fed a water wheel which powered the bellows.

What were the problems with windmills?

Windmills had been in existence for centuries, for pumping water, milling flour and sawing wood. Like water, this power source was affected by the weather, although there were attempts to improve windmills.

◀ **SOURCE 1**
Horse gin used for haulage, 1798.

In 1745 fantails were added to the back of the sails to make sure they always pointed into the wind. Cast iron parts, which were introduced after 1754 by John Smeaton, lasted a long time. By 1787, millwrights were able to control the speed of windmills by using a centrifugal governor. Once built, they were cheap to run – as long as there was enough wind. However, even large windmills could only produce about 15 horse power. A more reliable source of power was needed.

Was steam power the answer?

In 1698 a Captain Savery from Cornwall built a steam engine which could draw water out of a mine. As it had no safety valve, there was always the risk of it exploding. It failed to work very well, and there was clearly much more work for engineers to do before people were convinced that steam could provide the power they needed.

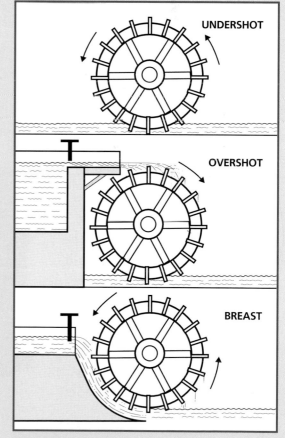

UNDERSHOT

OVERSHOT

BREAST

SOURCE 2
The different types of water wheel. ▲

6.2 How far did steam engine technology develop in the 18th century ?

The introduction of the steam engine

In 1706, Thomas Newcomen (1663-1729), a blacksmith from Devon, built his first atmospheric steam engine (Source 3). This noisy, wheezing monster could make the beam rise and fall 10 times a minute to pump 100 gallons of water out of a mine. By 1711, Newcomen was manufacturing these engines. In 1717 they were improved when Henry Beighton of Newcastle fitted a safety valve to prevent a dangerous build-up of steam.

Mine owners realised how useful these Newcomen engines could be and, gradually, more and more were built. By the 1770s, over 300 were in use. Unfortunately, they did not work very well.

● They used an enormous amount of coal because the cylinder was always being cooled down to condense the steam. Before the next stroke, it took more steam to heat the cylinder back up, otherwise there would be more condensation if the cylinder was cold.

● This wasted energy, but also meant that the beam did not work very fast.

● Steam was always escaping because the pistons fitted badly in the cylinder.

● The action of the beam was only up and down – no way had been found of making the beam turn a wheel.

KEY IDEAS

● Steam power increased the pace of the Industrial Revolution

● Newcomen's engine was inefficient

● Watt's separate condenser used less fuel

● The 'sun and planet gear' produced rotary motion

SOURCE 3
Newcomen's engine. ▼

How did James Watt help to improve the Newcomen engine?

James Watt (1736-1819) was the son of a skilled carpenter and shipwright from Greenock in Scotland. At a time when few people had any education at all, James went to grammar school. He went on to learn to be an instrument maker in London. By 1757 he was at Glasgow University where he earned his living making mathematical and musical instruments, as well as studying science.

In 1763 he was given a Newcomen engine to repair. His efforts to improve it took many years and were so expensive they nearly ruined him.

As Source 4 shows, Watt's engine had a separate condenser, which meant that heat was kept in the cylinder. It wasted less fuel. However, without capital, Watt was getting into debt.

Watt was then introduced to John Roebuck, the ironmaster who ran the Carron ironworks on Clydesdale. Roebuck needed an engine to help pump water from his mines, so he and Watt formed a partnership. In 1768 they made their first working engine, which they called Beelzebub. It did not work well. Once again, the parts did not fit well – especially the pistons inside the cylinder. To make matters worse, Roebuck was £1,200 in debt and went bankrupt in 1773.

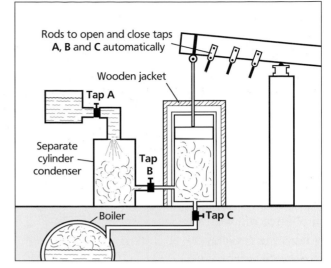

SOURCE 4 *Watt's separate condenser.* ▲

SOURCE 5 ▲

An artist's interpretation of the 'moment' when the young James Watt understood that steam could provide a source of power.

SOURCE 6

Matthew Boulton was keen to work with James Watt. He wrote to him in February 1769:

I was excited by two motives to offer you my assistance which were love of you and love of a money-getting project. I presumed that your engine would require money, very accurate workmanship and extensive correspondence to make it turn out to the best advantage. The best means of keeping up the reputation and doing the invention justice would be to keep the executive part out of the hands of the ordinary engineers who from ignorance, want of experience and want of necessary convenience, would be very liable to produce bad and inaccurate workmanship.

To remedy which and produce the most profit, my idea was to settle a manufactory near to my own by the side of our canal where I would erect all the conveniences necessary for the completion of engines, and from which manufactory we would serve all the world with engines of all sizes. With your assistance we could engage and instruct some excellent workmen, and could execute the invention 20 per cent cheaper, and with as great a difference of accuracy as there is between the blacksmith and the instrument-maker.

How important was Matthew Boulton to the development of the steam engine?

Matthew Boulton (1728-1809) was the owner of the Soho iron-making works in Birmingham. He had men with engineering skills, as well as capital, and was willing to take a chance on Watt's ideas. He took over Roebuck's debt, and became Watt's second partner. He moved the work from Scotland to Birmingham. Boulton was able to make better parts for Watt to use. An important step forward was the building of a machine to bore out cylinders so that pistons could fit them exactly. By 1775 they had a successful, working steam engine.

Unfortunately sales were so slow that Boulton got into serious debt. The engine could still only make a beam go up and down. The design was 'stolen' by other engineers who did not pay a royalty. Tin mines already used Newcomen's engine and, as they were not prospering, their owners did not want to invest in the new machine. Coal mine owners found it difficult to transport the engines to their mines, so stuck with the Newcomen engines they already had. Transporting the engines only became easier with the building of canals in the 1770s.

However, developments continued. By 1781, Watt and his works foreman, William Murdock, had built a 'sun and planet gear' which enabled the engine to turn a wheel (Source 7). With this rotary motion, the possibilities were now endless. Cotton mill owners wanted them to turn their machines. In 1785, the first textile mill took delivery – at Papplewick, near Nottingham. In 1782

SOURCE 7
Watt's engine with the 'sun and planet' gear.

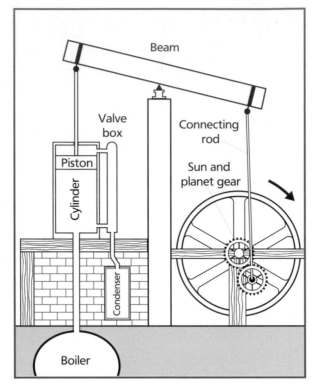

there were only 50 Watt engines in use. By 1800 there were 1,200. Steam was replacing water power. A revolution was at last about to take place in power supply.

There was a rush of other developments. In 1782 Watt's team had invented a way of forcing steam into the cylinder so it could push the piston upwards and then force it downwards too – it was double acting. By 1784, an engine was working the tilt hammers of an iron forge.

The advantages of Watt's engine, which could save a third of the fuel costs of a Newcomen engine, were obvious. It still took time for it to be completely adopted. But by the middle of the 19th century, Watt's engines were becoming commonplace in industrial Britain.

Questions

1. Why did (a) wind and (b) water not always provide reliable power for industry?

2. What were the drawbacks of Newcomen's engine?

3. What were the differences between Newcomen's and Watt's first engines?

4. Why was it difficult for Watt to develop and sell his early engines?

5. Who was the most important figure in the development of steam power: Newcomen, Boulton or Watt?

6.3 *How important was the steam engine to the Industrial Revolution?*

- At the iron foundry at Coalbrookdale steam engines pumped water so it could reach the bellows that blew air through the furnaces.
- Later, steam engines drove tilt hammers and rolling mills.
- Breweries, water works, and flour mills all relied on steam power.
- Steam drove the machines in cotton mills.
- Steam power relied on coal mining, but the engines helped to keep the mines free of flood water and to haul the coal to the surface.

- Eventually, steam was applied to transport. Steam enabled the Industrial Revolution to gather speed. Large-scale production processes were possible which increased the supply and lowered the price of, for instance, iron and cotton goods. It enabled industry to move away from countryside rivers to the towns where employment was found for the ever increasing population.

Steam was at the heart of the industrial development in the 19th century.

SOURCE 8
Some people thought steam power would lead to mass unemployment, as this cartoon shows.▼

Question

Why was steam so important to British industry in the 19th century?

WORKING CONDITIONS

7.1 *How bad were conditions in the factories and mines*

By the early 19th century, working conditions in mines and factories were causing concern. However, the illustration in Source 1 and the statement in Source 3 give us very different views of the lives of child workers. When historians see sources like these they have to ask 'who produced them and why?'

Reformers – people who wanted to make conditions better – wanted Parliament to pass Acts to protect workers. Between 1800 and 1853, Parliament set up several Royal Commissions to find out what working conditions were really like. Some people deliberately made things sound bad so that the Government would take action. Other people defended the employers by showing that working conditions were not so bad after all. However, the Royal Commissions collected evidence which showed that, in most cases, working conditions were shocking.

Factory working conditions

Child workers as young as 3 years old were employed. They worked long hours in dangerous conditions. Factory children's legs and backs were crooked from scrambling in cramped spaces underneath the machines. They received no education.

Hours were long. When the factory was especially busy, workers could be forced to work over 15 hours a day.

The **atmosphere** was kept hot and humid to prevent the threads from breaking. Workers breathed polluted air. Open toilet buckets allowed diseases, such as typhus, to spread through the air. Dust in the air irritated workers' lungs and caused chest complaints.

Machinery was dangerous. The moving parts were not covered. Children who were 'piecers' had to crawl under spinning machines to tie up threads if they snapped. It was easy for their fingers and limbs to get trapped and mangled in the moving parts.

Discipline was harsh. Strappers and overseers, who were paid according to the amount produced, beat the exhausted workers to make them work harder. Workers were made to pay fines for all kinds of reasons (see Source 2).

Wages were low. Employers paid women and children less than men. Payment was sometimes given as tokens. This was called the 'truck' system. Tokens could only be used at the employer's own shop. Food prices there were usually high, and the quality was low.

◄ **SOURCE 1**
A mother drags her exhausted child to the mill. An illustration from The Life and Adventures of Michael Armstrong the Factory Boy *by Frances Trollope.*

SOURCE 2

Factory rules:

1. The door of the mill will be closed ten minutes after the engine starts. Any weaver absent will be fined 3d per loom.
2. Weavers leaving the room without consent will be fined 3d.
3. All shuttles, brushes, oil-cans, wheels, if broken, will be paid for by the weaver.
4. If any hand is seen talking to another, whistling or singing, he will be fined 6d.

Mine working conditions

Hours were long, pay was low and conditions were worse than in factories. Women were a third of the workforce and children were also employed in the mines. The smallest children spent hours in the dark, opening and shutting the trap doors in the ventilation system. Older children and women dragged the coal to the bottom of the pitshaft in baskets, using chains fastened round their waists.

Working in a mine was **extremely dangerous**. Miners were killed by suffocating gas, gas explosions and flooding. Hauling the coal out of the mine using badly maintained ropes or ladders resulted in falls, or people being buried under coal or rock.

Other industries

Similar conditions were found in other industries such as brewing (see Source 4 page 70). Chimney sweeps used climbing boys to clean out soot-filled chimneys with their bare hands. In agriculture, women and children worked under the control of a gangmaster. Cruelty and beatings added to the discomforts of working every daylight hour in all weathers.

SOURCE 3

Dr Ure reported, in 1835, that he found that:

The child workers seemed always cheerful and alert ... As to exhaustion by the day's work they showed no trace of it on coming out of the mill in the evening they skip around any nearby playground.

What were people's attitudes to the reform of working conditions?

For reform: Reformers thought that the Government should pass laws to improve working conditions. They drew attention to the lack of any education for child workers. They were concerned about the harsh treatment workers received, and the state of 'slavery' which existed in Britain's industrial centres.

Some reformers were concerned about workers' morals. They questioned whether it was right for men and women, boys and girls, to work so closely together, particularly in the mines. They also argued that, with so many women going out to work, home and family life would fall apart.

Against reform: Like many people in the 19th century, employers held laissez-faire views. They thought that the Government had no right to interfere in the way they ran their businesses.

Employers believed that if workers' hours were cut, then profits would fall. They warned that, if profits fell, businesses might go bankrupt, and factories would close. This would mean that many workers lost their jobs, and unemployment would rise.

Employers thought that factories offered advantages to their workers. They said that wages were higher in the factories than under the Domestic System. They said that workers were used to long hours, and that earning their money through honest hard toil gave them self-respect. Employers defended child labour by saying that parents needed the money that their children earned. (It was true that, under the Domestic System, children had worked and contributed to the family income. However, they had worked with the family group, and their parents were responsible for discipline, unlike in the factory where the family was split up and overseers punished the children.)

Not everyone agreed that the factory system was cruel. Employers claimed that children only did light work in the warmth of a textile factory. Children were ideal 'piecers' – which meant they tied up the loose threads underneath the spinning machines. Dr Ure talked of these young workers being like 'little elves at play'.

SOURCE 4
Working conditions in a brewery, 1872.▼

7.2 How successful were attempts to reform working conditions?

Robert Owen – a reforming employer

Robert Owen (1771-1858) and his father-in-law owned a cotton mill at New Lanark in Scotland. When Owen took over the running of the mill in 1799, he decided to improve conditions for his workers:

- Good wages were paid.
- The working day was cut to $10^{1}/2$ hours maximum. This was a lot shorter than the normal working day in factories.
- If workers did not work, either because they were sick or because business was slack, they still received some pay.
- No children under 10-years-old were employed.

Other factory owners looked on in horror, because they were sure that Owen would be financially ruined by making these improvements. However, they were proved wrong. Owen's mills did not go bankrupt.

KEY IDEAS

- Robert Owen improved working conditions and still made a profit
- Early Factory Acts were ineffective
- The Ten Hours Movement tried to get Parliament to cut working hours
- The $10^{1}/2$ hour working day was won in 1853

Instead, they made a profit which Owen spent on creating better living conditions for his workers.

Owen built rows of 'model housing' with decent drains. This was so called because it was a 'model' that Owen wanted other people to copy. Owen rented the houses to his workers for a fair price. He also built schools (he understood the importance of education), grocery shops and a wash house. Hardly any employers copied him. Sir Titus Salt built a model village for employees at Saltaire in Yorkshire – but this was not until the 1850s.

In general, employers were not interested in Owen's reforms. Conditions remained shocking, and so reformers had to turn to Parliament to pass laws to protect workers.

SOURCE 5 ▲
The inside of a mill. The workers look neatly dressed and working conditions seem good.

The early Factory Acts

The **1802 and 1819 Factory Acts** (see Source 6) showed that the Government accepted some responsibility for working conditions. However, the Acts did not achieve much.

- There were no inspectors to make sure the Acts were obeyed.
- The Acts only applied to cotton mills, not woollen mills.
- Proving children's ages was difficult until the registration of births began in 1836. Parents (who needed the money) and employers (who needed cheap labour) lied about the ages of child workers.

These Acts disappointed Reformers. **The Ten Hours Movement** was set up to campaign for a shorter working day.

SOURCE 6 *The Factory Acts.*

Acts to reform working conditions

- **The 1802 Health and Morals of Apprentices Act:** Orphan apprentices were to work no more than 12 hours a day and not at night. They were to be given some schooling and two sets of clothes a year.
- **The 1819 Factory Act:** No children under 9 were to work. Children aged from 9 to 18 could work no more than 12 hours a day, and not at night.
- **The 1833 Factory Act:** No children under 9 were allowed to work. Children between 9 and 13 could only work up to 8 hours a day, and were to have 2 hours schooling a day. Young people between 14 and 18 were to work at most 12 hours a day. No one under 18 was to work nights. Four inspectors were appointed.
- **The 1842 Mines Act:** No females or boys under 10 were to work underground. Mines inspectors could visit the pits to ensure the Act was being obeyed.
- **The 1844 Factory Act:** Children aged 8 to 13 were to work no more than 7 hours a day. Young workers between 14 and 18, and women between 18 and 21 years had their hours cut to 69 a week. More inspectors were appointed.
- **The Ten Hours Act (1847):** This applied to young people and women.
- **The 1853 Factory Act:** The length of the working day was fixed at $10\frac{1}{2}$ hours. It lasted either from 6am until 6pm, or 7am to 7pm, with $1\frac{1}{2}$ hours for breaks.

Did the Ten Hours Movement succeed?

The Ten Hours Movement gathered pace in the 1830s. This was a period of great hardship because industry was affected by slumps in trade. There also seemed to be more people than ever living in a 'state of slavery', as Richard Oastler called it (see Source 7). There were an estimated 30,000 children under 13-years-old working in factories.

Two Tory MPs, Michael Sadler and the future Lord Shaftesbury (Anthony Ashley – 1801-85) tried to introduce Ten Hour Bills into Parliament. However, some MPs for industrial towns who had been elected by the factory owners did not like this. To slow things down they set up a Select Committee to collect evidence about working conditions (while the Committee was running, no changes would happen).

The witnesses who appeared before the Committee gave different views of working conditions, depending on whether they wanted reform or were against it. Even so, when the Committee published its evidence, the public was shocked. The Home Secretary responded to the outcry, and the **1833 Factory Act** was passed. The Act did not do enough:

- There were only four inspectors to make sure the Act was obeyed.
- Schools provided under the Act were poor.

SOURCE 7

Richard Oastler's letter to the Leeds Mercury *newspaper, 1830:*

Let the truth speak out. Thousands of our fellow-creatures, both male and female ... are at this very moment existing in a state of slavery more horrid than are the victims of that hellish system – 'Colonial Slavery'. Thousands of little children are daily compelled to labour from six in the morning to seven in the evening with only – Britons, blush whilst you read it! – with only thirty minutes for eating and recreation.

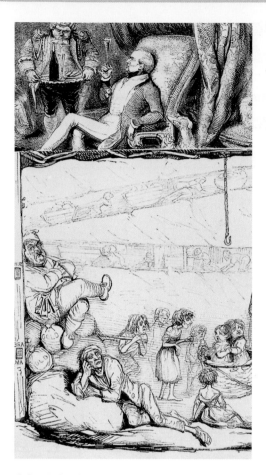

SOURCE 9

Two contrasting extracts from the 1842 Report of the Commission on the Labour of Women and Children in Mines.

(1) One of the men on the Commission wrote these notes about Nicol Hudderson, age 10 who worked in a colliery:

Is lame now, and will always be lame. The heat in the pit makes him sick. Is in very bad health. Feels worst when he goes down first at three o'clock in the morning. It is seven in the evening before he gets home sometimes. Seldom eats. Lies down by the fireside.

(2) Henry Morton, a mine agent, gave evidence for an owner:

The usual employment of children in coal mines is perfectly consistent with their health. They make very good wages. Working at night makes little difference, as the ventilation is the same at one period as at another.

Never heard of any boys straining themselves in these pits.

Any law which restricted children working would prevent many pits from being carried on.

SOURCE 8

A 19th century cartoon shows that while the miners are at work, the mine owner enjoys himself.

● Proving children's ages was still difficult. If a mill owner was taken to court, fines were often as low as £1. Many magistrates were also mill owners.

The **1844 Factory Act** and **1847 Ten Hours Act** cut the hours of children and women, but not those of men. Some people hoped that men would not be able to work long hours because, at times, there would be no women to run the machines. This did not happen because employers used relays of women working shifts. It was not until the **1853 Factory Act** that the $10^{1}/2$ hour working day was won.

The Mines Act

The 1842 Royal Commission revealed the appalling conditions suffered by women and children in the mines (Sources 8 and 9(1)). Shaftesbury was determined to change this. The result was the **1842 Mines Act** which stopped women, girls and young boys working in the mines. This made some female miners angry because, instead of working underground, they had to work at the pit head for lower wages. However, it was a difficult Act to enforce as inspectors were not allowed underground until 1850.

Questions

1. Do you think conditions in mines were worse than those in factories? Explain your answer. (Look back at pages 58-61.)

2. How reliable are Sources 8 and 9 to a historian studying 19th century working conditions?

3. How accurate was Oastler's view of factory conditions (Source 7)?

4. How important was Robert Owen to the factory reform movement?

5. Why were early Factory Acts ineffective?

6. What were the important reasons as to why working conditions had improved by 1853?

8 TRANSPORT: ROADS

8.1 *What were roads like in the early 1700s*

A journey by road in 1700 could be expensive, uncomfortable and even dangerous. In 1700 most roads in Britain were in a poor state of repair. Many were only cart tracks (Source 1). The Romans had been the last great road builders in England. People still used Roman roads but, after more than a thousand years, they were in poor condition. Repairs consisted of little more than filling the worst of the potholes and ruts with stones.

The soft surfaces of roads quickly became a sea of mud in wet weather. In winter the mud froze into ruts. In summer the roads became dry, cracked and dusty. Deep potholes could make vehicles overturn, sometimes causing fatal accidents. Tracks were narrow, littered with boulders and obstacles. Many roads and tracks were overhung by trees that provided cover for highwaymen. There was no artificial lighting, and, unless the moon was full, it was difficult and dangerous to travel at night.

Arthur Young, the agricultural journalist and traveller, often commented on the state of the roads around the country. He complained about one road in southern England, *'it is so narrow that a mouse cannot pass by any carriage. The ruts are an incredible depth. Trees overgrow the road keeping out the sun'*. One road near Wigan in Lancashire was so bad that travellers were warned to avoid it *'as they would the devil'*.

What kinds of traffic used the roads?

At the beginning of the 18th century goods were carried by slow, heavy **stage-waggons** which were pulled by pairs of horses. These could travel no faster than two miles per hour. If the roads were too bad for wheeled vehicles, pack horses (Source 2) and mule trains were used instead.

It was difficult to transport bulky goods such as coal, because one horse could only carry about 125 kilograms. Transport costs made coal too expensive for anyone living more than 15 miles from a mine.

SOURCE 1 ▲
An 18th-century drawing of a road.

Stage-coaches carried passengers around the country but these were slow, travelling no more than about 30 miles per day. Journeys were also expensive.

Roads were not just used by vehicles. Some people rode on horseback. Others, like pedlars, walked from one village or town to another. Sometimes people joined together in large groups for safety. It was not uncommon to see herds of sheep and cattle, and even flocks of geese, being driven along the poor roads to far-off markets for sale.

Why did Britain need good roads?

The poor state of the roads was a serious problem. Roads were important for good communication which was necessary for Britain to develop successfully, and for industry to become strong economically. Without the ability to transport goods and people efficiently, cheaply and reliably, industry would not prosper. Britain needed good roads.

SOURCE 2 ▲
A pack-horse.

8.2 Why were roads in 18th-century Britain so bad ?

Who repaired the roads?

In the early 18th century, maintenance of each road was the responsibility of the villagers and farmers who used it. This had been the custom since the middle ages. But at that time roads were mostly used by people that lived near-by. It was fair that they should have responsibility for road repairs. However, by the 16th century it was obvious that some roads were being used more by people from further away.

The parish system of road repair (statute labour)

As the amount of traffic increased, villagers found themselves mending roads, not just for their own benefit, but also for travellers who had nothing to do with the village. Many parish authorities were reluctant to force people to work on the roads. They protested that it was through traffic, rather than local traffic, that damaged the roads. But in 1555 their protests were rejected by an Act of Parliament called **The Statute for Mending the Highways** which made each parish responsible for the upkeep of its own roads.

Under this system:
• Each parish had to elect two unpaid surveyors.
• Villagers were required to do four (later increased to six) days unpaid labour per year on road repair.
• Those who earned over £50 a year had to supply materials and tools free of charge.
• Magistrates had to ensure that the work was carried out properly.

> ### KEY IDEAS
> • The parish was responsible for the roads in its area
> • Parish system did little to improve roads
> • Government showed little interest in roads

SOURCE 3
Road menders working under the parish system of road repair.
▼

As Source 4 shows the system did little to improve the state of the roads. Why?

• The surveyors (and villagers) were unpaid, and knew little about road mending.
• Most repairs consisted of tipping stones into the ruts and potholes.
• Villagers had their own jobs which they resented leaving for six days, (although many treated the work as a holiday).
• There was a lack of funds which limited the materials available for repair.
• They did not have the correct tools to carry out the work.

Was Government interested in the roads?

The Government showed little interest in the state of the roads in the early 18th century. There were, however, two occasions when it decided to take action.

In the 1720s and 1730s the Government was worried that there would be an uprising of the Highland Clans. To make sure that the army could move quickly around southern Scotland, the Government ordered **General Wade** to build 200 miles of road, which he did between 1726 and 1737. He built some of his roads up to 10 metres wide with strong foundations. These improvements enabled Wade to move his troops rapidly to trouble spots. However, these roads had little effect on the main areas of population.

The Government again showed an interest in roads several years later. Because broad wheels were believed to do less damage to the road surface than other types, the Government passed the **Broad Wheels Act** in 1753. Goods waggons were required to have wheels at least 23 cm wide (Source 5). This Act did little to improve the state of the roads.

The Government was reluctant to take direct responsibility for roads, but an effective system was still needed to improve Britain's roads.

SOURCE 4

Although road mending was a duty of the parish and the community, few people wanted to perform it. This resulted in comments like these:

When a man is called to perform statute work, he goes reluctantly; his servants and his horses seem to partake of his laziness. The surveyor cannot rouse them and the work done is less than half what it ought to be.

From a survey of the operation of statute labour in Somerset, 1798.

Sometimes the worst horses are sent, at others a broken cart, or a boy, or an old man who is past heavy work. They are sometimes sent an hour or two too late in the morning, or they leave off much sooner than the proper time.

The Complete Farmer, *1807.*

They make a holiday of it, lounge about and trifle away their time. As they are in no danger of being turned out of their work, they stand in no awe of the Surveyor.

St. James's Chronicle, *5 January 1768.*

They know not how to lay foundations, nor to make the proper slopes or drains. They pour a heap of loose, huge stones into a swampy hole which make the best of their way to the centre of the earth.

Gentleman's Magazine, *1752.*

SOURCE 5
An 18th-century wide-wheeled waggon. ▶

Questions

1. Describe the problems faced by people using roads in the 18th century (use pages 74-75).

2. Why were the roads in such a poor condition?

3. Look at Source 3. What can you learn from this source about the parish system of road repair?

4. Explain why the parish system did not improve roads.

5. (a) What did the Government do to improve roads?
   (b) How successful was the Government?

6. How useful is the interpretation in Source 1 (pages 74-75) to a historian studying early 18th-century transport?

8.3 *How successful were Turnpike Trusts in improving Britain's roads*?

Industry needed good roads

The Government was reluctant to do anything about improving roads, and it was obvious that the parish system could not provide good roads. The pressure to improve the roads came from the newly developing industries.

- Industry needed improved communications systems, such as the delivery of mail.
- Industry needed cheap and regular supplies of raw materials, such as cotton, coal and iron ore. These had to be carried to where they were needed.
- Finished products, such as cloth, had to be taken to markets around the country or to ports for export abroad.
- There was an increasing need to carry food from the countryside to feed the fast growing population in the towns.

An early answer to the problem of poor road conditions were the Turnpike Trusts.

SOURCE 6
A 20th-century photograph of an 18th century toll-house.▼

Turnpike Trusts

From 1663 onwards, groups of local people, usually gentry and merchants, paid for private Acts of Parliament giving them the right to form a trust and permission to raise money to build, or improve, stretches of main road. These groups were called Turnpike Trusts. A turnpike was a gate built at each end of a road that the Trust maintained. By the gate was a toll-house (see Source 6), at which road users had to stop and pay a fee (called a toll) to the trustees. The cost of the toll

SOURCE 7

The weather was bitterly cold; a great deal of snow fell from time to time, and the wind was intolerably keen. They were a little way out of Grantham when Nicholas was suddenly aroused by a violent jerk. He found that the coach had sunk down on one side. The vehicle then turned over.

A stage-coach journey described in Charles Dickens' novel Nicholas Nickleby, *1839.*

SOURCE 8

These were the tolls at Llanfair Gate in the 19th century:

For every Horse, Mule or other Cattle, drawing any Coach or other Carriage with springs the sum of 4d.

For every Horse, Mule or other Beast or Cattle drawing any Waggon Cart or other such Carriage not employed solely in carrying or going empty to fetch Lime for manure the sum of 3d.

For every Horse, Mule, or other Beast or Cattle drawing any Waggon, Cart or other such Carriage employed solely in carrying or going empty to fetch Lime for Manure the sum of 1$\frac{1}{2}$d.

For every Horse Mule or Ass laden or unladen and not drawing, the sum of 1d.

For every Horse, Mule or other Beast drawing any Waggon or Cart, the Wheels being less than 3 inches in breadth or having Wheels with Tires fastened with Nails projecting and not countersunk to pay double Toll.

What were the problems of turnpikes?

● There was no national system. Trusts were competing against each other.
● Not all roads were covered by a Turnpike Trust.
● It was a costly system because passing the Act through Parliament was expensive, and toll collectors had to be paid.
● Some Trusts were dishonest or badly managed, and failed to spend the tolls on improving the roads.
● Toll collectors could be bribed for less than the toll.
● Travellers did not like paying tolls.
● Tolls could make travel more expensive.
● There were delays at the gates.
● Local people objected to paying to use roads that previously had been free of charge, and sometimes this led to riots.

varied depending on the type of vehicle (see Source 8). The Trust used the tolls to pay for improvements to their stretch of road and to employ an engineer to take responsibility for the improvements.

By 1838, out of almost 130,000 miles of road, 22,000 miles were the responsibility of the Trusts, while the remainder were still under parish responsibility. There was a good network of main roads out of London. Under the Turnpike Trusts, roads throughout Britain began to improve.

What were the benefits of turnpikes?

● The number of well-surfaced, well-drained roads increased.
● Roads were wider, straighter and with gentle gradients.
● Some isolated towns and villages were linked.
● Wheeled traffic increased.
● A mail service was introduced in 1784.
● Improved roads made it easier and cheaper to transport goods.

However, despite these problems, travelling conditions improved a lot.

YORK Four Days Stage-Coach.

Begins on Friday *the* 12th. *of* April. 1706.

ALL that are desirous to pass from *London* to *York*, or from *York* to *London*, or any other Place on that Road; Let them Repair to the *Black Swan* in *Holbourn* in *London*, and to the *Black Swan* in *Coney* street in *York*.

At both which Places, they may be received in a Stage Coach every *Monday*, *Wednesday* and *Friday*, which performs the whole Journey in Four Days, (if God permits,) And sets forth at Five in the Morning.

And returns from *York* to *Stamford* in two days, and from *Stamford* by *Huntington* to *London* in two days more. And the like Stages on their return.

Allowing each Passenger 14l. weight, and all above 3d a Pound.

Performed By { Benjamin *Kingman*, Henry *Harrison*, Walter *Baynes*.

Also this gives Notice that *Newcastle* Stage Coach, sets out from *York*, every *Monday*, and *Friday*, and from *Newcastle* every *Monday* and *Friday*.

SOURCE 9

Poster advertising a stage-coach journey in 1706. ▲

Mail-coaches

In 1784 John Palmer of Bath introduced the carrying of the Royal Mail by coach between London and Bristol. These mail-coaches had an armed-guard for protection. Their journeys were faster because Mail-coaches did not have to stop at the toll-gates. They also carried passengers.

The 'Golden Age' of coaching

The period between 1820 and 1840 became known as the 'Golden Age' of coaching. (A nostalgia about this era is often shown in coaching scenes on Christmas cards.) The express stage-coaches travelling out of London were able to average ten to twelve miles per hour. This speed was partly due to changing the horses regularly during the journey at the coaching inns along the main roads. (Coaching inns sprang-up to meet the growing needs of the transport system.) The stage-coaches were improved to make them more comfortable for passengers. Despite the more regular services, travel by coach remained expensive. (In 1832 the journey from Manchester to London was £4. 4s – £4.20).

What was a stage coach journey like?

● The journey usually started and finished at an inn.
● The fare depended on whether you travelled inside, or outside where you were exposed to all the bad weather.
● Although the coach had springs it was still uncomfortable as the seats were not padded and there was no heating.

SOURCE 10 ▲
A traditional Christmas card.

● Stops were made at coaching inns to change the horses. This was an opportunity for the travellers to get something to eat.

Questions

1. Why was there a need to improve roads?

2. Describe how Turnpike Trusts were set up.

3. Why were many toll-houses similar in shape to the one shown in Source 6?

4. Why did the mail-coach not have to stop and pay a toll?

5. Describe a stage-coach journey.

6. How far did turnpikes improve road travel?

7. The Christmas card (source 10) is a modern interpretation of 19th century travel.
   (a) Explain what a historian might learn from the card
   (b) How useful is this interpretation to a historian?

8.4

Did the great road engineers achieve anything ?

To build good roads required the special knowledge of engineers. Three men played key roles in improving Britain's roads by using new techniques. These men were John Metcalf, Thomas Telford and John Macadam.

KEY IDEAS

- Metcalf introduced drainage

- Telford developed a solid foundation for roads

- Macadam created a compact waterproof road surface

John Metcalf (1717-1810)
- Blinded by smallpox at the age of six.
- Nicknamed 'Blind Jack of Knaresborough'.
- Built three miles of the Harrogate to Boroughbridge turnpike road in 1763.
- He paid special attention to drainage.
- Used heather as a foundation on the Huddersfield to Manchester road in 1782 as he had to build the road over marshy ground.
- He retired at the age of 75 having built over 180 miles of turnpike road, mainly in Lancashire, Yorkshire and Derbyshire.
- His work helped to speed up the Industrial Revolution in these areas by improving the transportation of raw materials and finished products.
- He was responsible for the first good roads to be built in Britain since the Romans.

SOURCE 11

As he had been engaged to make nine miles of road in ten months he began in six different parts with almost four hundred men. One of the places was a deep bog. Numbers of clothiers passing that way held differing thoughts about how long it would take. He ordered sixty men to pull and bind heather in round bundles and to lay it on the intended road in rows and place another row across and pressing well down. He then used broad wheeled carriages, carts and waggons to bring stone or gravel for covering. This piece of road needed no repairs for twelve years after.

From a biography of John Metcalf, published in 1812, based on the engineer's recollections late in his life.

◄ **SOURCE 12**
John Metcalf.

Thomas Telford (1757-1834)
- A Scottish stonemason.
- In 1787 appointed surveyor of public works in Shropshire.
- Built his roads with a solid foundation, which made them expensive but long lasting. The firm surface was cambered (slightly curved) to allow the rain to drain off.
- He stressed the need to avoid sharp bends, and keep gradients gentle.
- He built nearly 1,000 miles of road as well as 100 bridges in Scotland.
- He built many bridges using cast iron.
- He built the London to Holyhead road (now the A5) for the Post Office and to enable Irish MPs to get to Westminster more easily.
- The road was opened in 1826 and reduced the journey time from London to Holyhead to 27 hours.
- This road features his famous Menai suspension bridge linking mainland Wales to Anglesey. He also built the Conwy suspension bridge.
- He built roads in the Shropshire area to help the growing iron industry around Ironbridge.
- He was responsible for building the Glasgow to Carlisle road that was completed in 1814 and which improved communications between Scotland and England.

The plan is this. First to level and drain. Then like the Romans, to lay a solid pavement of large stones for the foundation, the round or broad ends as close together as possible. The points are then broken off. A layer of very small stones is laid over them so that the whole are bound together. On top of this is laid gravel if it is available. The road is made as near perfect as possible.

A contemporary description by Robert Southey, a poet, of the work of his friend Thomas Telford.

Thomas Telford.

Telford's Conwy suspension bridge in North Wales.

The results of road improvements

The improvements in roads meant faster travel for people and letters. This was a great help in building up businesses around the country. Josiah Wedgwood, the great potter, took the opportunity to set up a network of travelling salesmen so that his pottery could be sold across Britain. There was an increase in the amount of fruit and vegetables coming into London which could be brought in from a wider area. In rural areas lime, marl and manure were carried over shorter distances. The changes, however, made less impact on the transportation of bulky goods. It remained far too expensive to carry these by road. These still required the development of other forms of transport.

It is important not to exaggerate the improvements that took place in road building during the 18th and early 19th centuries. In 1815, it was estimated that less than 1,000 miles of highway had been improved using the methods of Metcalf, Telford or Macadam. However, by 1815 Britain did have a national network of serviceable roads connecting most parts of the country. Even so, by 1836, when the number of roads maintained by Turnpike Trusts reached its peak of nearly 22,000 miles, there were still around 106,000 miles under parish control.

The importance of the roads declined with the development of the railways. Railways were cheaper, quicker and more comfortable for passenger travel. By about 1850, railways had reached most of the country, and stage-coach travel had almost disappeared. With the fall in traffic, most Turnpike Trusts went bankrupt. Roads were taken over by local authorities, and the Trusts disappeared.

John Loudon Macadam (1756-1836)

- Surveyor of Turnpike Trusts in London and Bristol (1815).
- Stressed the need for a good surface rather than expensive heavy foundations, making his roads cheaper than Telford's.

- He used small chips of granite that were ground down by the metal rims of wheeled-traffic to form a compact waterproof surface. This basic idea is still used today but now tar is added to the top layer.
- More than 1,000 miles of roads were constructed under his supervision. He published his methods and they were widely copied.
- He became Surveyor General of the Metropolitan Turnpike Trust and, partly through his influence, the General Highways Act was passed in 1835. This repealed the Act of 1555 and allowed parishes to raise local rates for the upkeep of the roads.

SOURCE 16

◄ *John Loudon Macadam.*

SOURCE 17

Thomas de Quincey, an author and critic wrote at the time:

It is in reality to Mr Macadam that we owe it all. The roads in England, within a few years, have been remodelled upon principles of Roman science. From mere beds of rivers and systems of ruts, they have been improved universally to the condition and appearance of gravel walks in private parks.

SOURCE 18

M. de Saussure, a French visitor described the state of the roads about 1725:

The roads are magnificent being wide, smooth and well kept. In this country everyone who makes use of the roads is obliged to contribute to the cost of keeping them. At equal distances there are gates called 'turnpikes', where you have to pay.

SOURCE 19

This day an inquest was held on the body of Richard Aimes, when it appeared that the deceased was thrown from his horse and was suffocated by mud and filth.

The Ipswich Journal, *18 March 1769.*

Questions

1. Complete a table giving three reasons why each of the great road engineers were important.

2. How much had road travel improved by 1815?

3. (a) In what ways do Source 18 and Source 19 differ in their comments on road travel?
   (b) Give reasons for their differences.
   (c) Is the fact that they give different versions of the state of the roads mean that they are of no use to a historian?

4. The following contributed to improving the road system:
   General Wade;
   John Metcalf;
   John Macadam;
   Thomas Telford.
   Were any of these more important than the others?

5. If Metcalf, Telford and Macadam only improved 1,000 miles of roads by 1815, were they really important to the development of road travel?

9 TRANSPORT: WATER

9.1 *How important was water transport in the early 18th century*

THIS SECTION ANSWERS:

9.1 *How important was water transport in the early 18th century?*

9.2 *What changed in water transport?*

9.3 *How difficult was canal building?*

9.4 *Were canals a success?*

SOURCE 1
A picture of a river being used to transport goods. ▼

In the early 18th century, the sea and rivers were used for the carriage of bulky goods such as coal, grain and building materials. They had advantages over road transport, which was slow and expensive.

Transport by sea

For centuries ships had carried goods around the coasts. Coal was a particularly important cargo. Demand for coal to heat homes had been increasing steadily, and it was also used in making glass, bricks and beer. The main coal-field was on Tyneside, in the north-east of England. Coal was taken from there to London by sea – it became known as **sea-coal**. However, because the weather could affect sailing conditions, delivery times were uncertain. Boats could even sink.

Transport by river

Sea transport alone could not meet the needs of trade inside Britain. Before 1750, merchants also used rivers such as the Severn, Trent and Thames to transport heavy and bulky goods such as coal and grain. Unfortunately for the merchants, not all rivers were suitable for transporting goods because:

- Rivers were too shallow.
- They had weirs, sandbanks, waterwheels and low bridges.
- They were long and winding.
- They did not flow where water transport was needed.
- The currents were too strong.

In fact, some rivers were 'improved' by digging out the river bed to make a constant depth and by cutting out meanders. These improved rivers became known as **navigations**. Improved rivers included the Mersey (Manchester and Liverpool) and Irwell (Manchester), the Weaver (Cheshire), the Aire and Calder (Leeds and Wakefield) and the Don (Sheffield).

KEY IDEAS

- Sea transport was unreliable

- River transport could not serve the whole country

- Another form of transport was needed

This work was financed by people who thought they would benefit from it, such as the cloth merchants of Leeds and Wakefield. They claimed *'it will mean a great increase in trade if goods can be sent by water. Many times the goods receive considerable damage through the badness of the roads by overturning'*.

However, John Smeaton, a Yorkshire canal engineer, was critical. He wrote in 1771, *'It seems to me that the men who thought up the idea of the river navigation had no idea how much trade was likely to be carried. Their plan was on too small a scale. The water is not deep enough. The men who designed the river navigation were also not aware that millers who owned water mills drew off water to power their machinery. The river navigation has always been under difficulties for these reasons.'*

SOURCE 2

Here is a great corn market, and great quantities of corn are brought here, and carried down by barges and other boats to Lynn. By these navigable rivers the merchants of Lynn supply about six counties in part with their goods, specially wine and coal.

Daniel Defoe, A Tour thro' the whole island of Great Britain, *1724-1726.*

What sort of transport was needed?

Although water transport existed, it did not meet all Britain's needs. A transport system was required that covered the whole country, could take heavy loads and was not too expensive. Although roads covered a lot of Britain they were too slow and expensive for transporting heavy, bulky goods. Transport by sea and by navigable river could not serve the whole country. Some towns were too far inland from the sea. Some areas, such as the industrial Midlands, needed to bring in raw materials and take out finished products but did not have navigable rivers.

9.2 What changed in water transport ?

As the natural system of waterways was not enough to meet Britain's transport needs **canals,** an artificial system of waterways, were developed.

The Sankey Brook Navigation

The first modern British canal was opened in 1757. This was the Sankey Brook Navigation between St. Helens and the River Mersey in Lancashire. This canal enabled coal from the St. Helens coalfield to be transported via the Mersey to Liverpool and Cheshire salt to be brought to Lancashire. The canal was mainly financed by local salt merchants. It proved to be a great success and merchants in South Lancashire realised that by transporting goods by canal they could make large profits.

James Brindley and the Worsley Canal

Francis Egerton, the 3rd Duke of Bridgewater owned a coal-mine at Worsley, seven miles from Manchester. He needed to drain his mines which were often flooded, and also to reduce the price he charged for his coal in Manchester. So at Bridgewater's request, in 1759 an Act of Parliament was passed to enable *'a navigable cut or canal to be made from Worsley Mill, over the River Irwell, to the town of Manchester'*. Bridgewater employed James Brindley, an illiterate millwright, as foreman engineer for a guinea (£1.05) per week. Brindley designed the canal to go straight into the mines at the Worsley end (helping to

KEY IDEAS

- Canal building began
- Manufacturers invested in canals
- James Brindley was an important canal builder

SOURCE 3
Brindley's Aqueduct at Barton. ▼

drain the mines), and to be carried over the River Irwell on an aqueduct at Barton. The canal allowed one horse to pull on water what it took 60 packhorses to carry. This reduced

SOURCE 4
James Brindley. ▼

the price of coal in Manchester by 50%, to 3d per ton. People bought more of Bridgewater's cheaper coal. Factory owners bought it in huge quantities, and the factory workers were able to buy cheaper coal to heat their homes. In 1776 the canal was extended to Runcorn on the Mersey, making a link between the Manchester cotton industry and the Port of Liverpool. The cost of transporting raw cotton and cotton goods between Liverpool and Manchester was reduced by 83%.

The Trent and Mersey Canal

The Worsley Canal was not James Brindley's only achievement. At a meeting in Staffordshire in December 1765, Brindley was asked to explain his plans for the Trent and Mersey Canal to Josiah Wedgwood. Wedgwood was most impressed by Brindley's idea. He knew how much his trade had suffered as a result of poor roads and rivers. He knew how it might grow if a canal linked Liverpool, Hull and Bristol. The meeting decided to ask Parliament for an Act allowing the canal to be built. Wedgwood contributed £1,000 to the scheme and promised to buy a large number of shares in the canal.

In 1766, Brindley was able to begin the Trent and Mersey Canal – his most ambitious scheme. It provided a continuous waterway from coast to coast across Britain. The canal ran from near Runcorn, through the salt and pottery districts of Cheshire and Staffordshire, to the Trent from where the river was navigable all the way to the Humber estuary. The canal was finished in 1777 with the opening of the Harecastle Tunnel. There was no towpath through this tunnel, so the bargees had the tiring task '**legging**' the barges. (They lay on their backs and used their feet to 'walk' along the tunnel wall.)

Unfortunately Brindley never saw the canal completed as he died in 1772. His death was of no surprise to his friends. Five years earlier Wedgwood had said, *'I am afraid he will do too much, and leave us before his vast designs are executed'.*

James Brindley (1716-1772)
- Born at Tunstead near Buxton in Derbyshire.
- His father was a labourer.
- In his early teens he worked as a farm labourer.
- When he was 17 he was apprenticed to a Macclesfield millwright.
- Being a poor writer, he developed a good memory for details.
- His work established him as the leading canal engineer of his time.
- If he had an engineering problem he retired to bed to think it through.
- Where possible he tried to follow the contours rather than use locks.
- He used the idea of puddled clay.
- The strain of building 365 miles of canal resulted in his death, aged 56.

Why did Wedgwood help to finance the Trent and Mersey Canal?

- He was able to transport Cornish china clay to his works after it had been brought round the coast to Liverpool.
- His finished pottery could be transported by barge with fewer breakages than by pack-horse.
- He was able to build his Etruria pottery works on the banks of the canal.

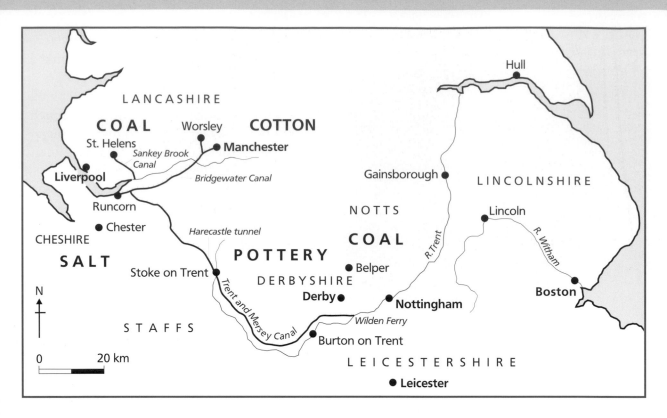

'Canal mania'

By 1790, the hub of the canal system – the area around Birmingham – was linked by water to Liverpool, Hull, London and Bristol.

Canals were very expensive to build. The Duke of Bridgewater calculated the cost at £10,000 per mile. Despite this, many new schemes were put forward, and between 1790 and 1797 there was a rush to invest in the profitable business of canal transport. By 1800, over 3,000 miles of canals had been completed.

Not all the schemes were as sound as the investors were led to believe.

SOURCE 6
Starvationers (very narrow boats) at the entrance to the mines at Worsley. ▼

◄ **SOURCE 7**
The northern end of the Harecastle Tunnels.

Some canals that were planned were never built. Others, particularly in agricultural areas in the south of England, lost money and eventually fell into disuse.

During this period of canal mania the Grand Junction Canal – which ran from London to Birmingham – and the Kennet and Avon Canal – which linked the Severn and the Thames – were started. Thomas Telford, the famous road engineer became involved in canal building towards the end of the period of canal mania with the Ellesmere Canal being completed in 1805, and the Caledonian Canal in Scotland in 1822. Unlike earlier canals – which kept costs low by following the contours of the land – the later ones often involved expensive engineering works.

SOURCE 8
Artist's impression of the Harecastle Tunnel. ▼

Questions

1. What problems did the users of rivers face when trying to move goods around the country? (Look at pages 84 and 85.)

2. Why was it not possible to improve river transport?

3. What advantages did the canal system bring to:
   (a) a mill owner in Manchester;
   (b) people living in Manchester;
   (c) industrialists like Bridgewater and Wedgwood?

4. Describe and illustrate the role of James Brindley in canal development.

5. Why were many people eager to invest in the building of canals?

6. Look at the two illustrations of the Harecastle Tunnel (Sources 7 and 8). How useful are these to a historian studying the development of canals?

7. Explain why some canals built in the south of England were not successful.

89

9.3 *How difficult was canal building* ?

KEY IDEAS

Problems and solutions were:

Hills and valleys:
- locks
- tunnels
- embankments

Rivers:
- aqueducts

Loss of water:
- puddled clay – clay mixed with water

Shortage of water:
- diversion of streams
- feeder reservoirs

Lack of labour:
- special working teams known as 'navvies'

Builders of canals faced many problems. These were often solved by expensive engineering works. Solutions included: **locks** (using water trapped between two gates to raise the water level and lift barges up); **embankments** (building up the level of the ground); and **aqueducts** (special bridges to carry water).

SOURCE 9

Another important navigation was the Rochdale Canal. This was built to open up a direct water communication between the manufacturing districts of West Yorkshire and South Lancashire. It would avoid the winding route of the Leeds and Liverpool Canal.

In one place a cutting fifty feet deep had to be blasted through hard rock. In other places it was overhung by precipices. In other places there was only room for the canal and turnpike road.

Large reservoirs had to be built to store water for summer droughts as well as to supply the numerous mills along the valley below.

Samuel Smiles, Lives of Engineers, *1862.*

SOURCE 10 ▲
Bingley Five Rise lock on the Leeds and Liverpool Canal.

Question

What difficulties faced the builders of the early canals? How were these difficulties overcome?

9.4 *Were canals a success* ?

KEY IDEAS

Canals:

- benefited industry
- lowered transport costs
- created employment
- suffered competition from railways

Benefits of canals

Canals brought many benefits, particularly to industry, as they were able to carry goods that could not be moved by road.

- Costs were reduced. A horse could pull twenty times more on a canal than on a good road.
- Canals were ideal for transporting goods for which speed was not important, such as raw cotton, coal, china clay and building materials.
- They helped agriculture by carrying lime, manure and grain.
- Some investors made large sums of money.
- Towns such as Stourport sprang up on the route.
- Canals were a source of employment. Many of the canals were built by navvies (navigators) often from Ireland. Later men were needed to handle the barges and their cargoes.

SOURCE 11

In 1782 a writer of the time gave his views of the benefits canals brought to Cheshire:

Instead of being covered in thatch, cottages are now covered with tiles or slates brought from Wales or Cumberland. The fields which were barren are now drained; by covering them with manure, carried on the canals, they have become green and fertile. Places which rarely obtained coal now have plentiful cheap supplies. The carrying of corn is easier than in past ages.

- There was no organised, planned canal system. Some canals and locks were different sizes and widths.
- Tolls on canals were often high, increasing the cost of goods.
- Canals were not suited to passenger traffic as they were too slow.
- Goods were often left on wharves where there was greater risk of theft.

Decline of canals

The golden age of canals lasted until about 1840 when railway competition became too great. Many canal companies sold out to the new railway companies which then allowed the canals to fall into disrepair.

- Railways were much faster. Often locks caused long delays and it was not unusual to see queues of boats waiting to pass through (see Source 16).
- Railways were more reliable, as canals often froze in winter and ran short of water in summer.

SOURCE 12

In 1824 a group of businessmen pointed out the problems of canals in the prospectus for the Liverpool and Manchester Railway:

In summertime, there is often a shortage of water, so boats go half-loaded. In winter they are often locked-up with frost for weeks on end. Sometimes goods take more than 21 days to get from Liverpool to Manchester. By the railroads, coal will be brought to market in greater quantity and at a reduced price. Farming produce will travel greater distances and travellers can be carried.

SOURCE 13

In 1804 Thomas Telford wrote:

It will be found that canals are chiefly useful for the following purposes: first, for conveying the produce of mines to the sea-shore; second, conveying fuel and raw materials to some manufacturing towns and districts and exporting the manufactured goods; third, conveying groceries for consumption of the district through which the canal passes, fourth conveying fuel for domestic purposes and manure for the purposes of agriculture.

SOURCE 14

Over 200 years later a modern historian wrote:

Canals helped agriculture. Barges carried grain and took loads of manure from the towns into the countryside. However, it is likely that canals only benefited those farms near their banks. No canal prospered that ran through rural areas only. Canals helped the building trade carrying sand, bricks and timber but as with farming it is unlikely that they served more than their immediate area. Buildings in the 18th century were made of local materials.

SOURCE 15 ▼
Figures for the Thames and Severn Canal. They show how many days the canal was closed in different years and why.

SOURCE 16 ▲
Coal boats waiting to pass over the Barton Aqueduct.

Year	By frost	For maintenance	Other reasons	Total days
1822	0	127	–	127
1826	20	26	70	116
1830	40	5	35	80

Questions

1. Describe the benefits of canals to farmers.

2. How did the use of canals help industrial growth before 1830?

3. What were the advantages of canals over (a) roads and (b) navigable rivers?

4. Look at Sources 11, 13 and 14. Source 14 gives a different view of the value of canals. Does this mean it is of little use?

5. The following are reasons why canals declined: lack of a planned network; slowness; impact of the weather; the coming of the railways.

   Which of these is the most important reason for the decline of canals?

10 TRANSPORT: RAILWAYS

10.1 *Why did the early railways develop* ?

KEY IDEA
- Canals and roads did not meet all Britain's transport needs

THIS SECTION ANSWERS:

10.1 *Why did the early railways develop?*

10.2 *What contribution did the Stephensons and Brunel make to railways?*

10.3 *How difficult was it for the railway system to grow?*

10.4 *What was the impact of railways?*

Problems of existing transport

Canals were not suitable for carrying perishable goods or for transporting people. Road travel had improved, although this was still relatively expensive. Another form of transport that was quicker, cheaper and more reliable was needed. The development of a national railway network, capable of carrying both goods and passengers, was to have a dramatic effect on industry, agriculture, people and other forms of transport.

Origins and early railway development

By about 1800 **waggonways**, **tramways** or **railed-ways** were common. The earliest tracks, built on the coalfields were simple wooden rails along which trucks were pulled by a horse. Cast-iron rails which could carry more than wooden ones became more popular in the late 1760s. In 1767 a cast-iron track was laid from Coalbrookdale to the Severn. It was recorded that *'one waggon with three horses will bring as much as 20 horses used to bring'*. The rail had a flange (a raised edge) to keep the wheel on the line. Later the flange was put on the wheel. In some areas there were stationary steam engines which used ropes, or wires, to haul waggons up a slope. There was 300 miles of track in Britain by 1810, most of it serving the coalfields. During the wars with France, horse power became more expensive because horses were required by the army. A cheaper substitute for moving goods along the tracks was needed.

SOURCE 1 ▲
A horse-drawn waggon being used to transport coal.

10.2 *What contribution did the Stephensons and Brunel make to railways* **?**

The Stockton and Darlington Railway

For a number of years the colliery owners around Darlington had been searching for a quicker and cheaper method of transporting their coal to the port of Stockton. They were led by a Quaker businessman called Edward Pease. Parliament granted permission, and Pease appointed George Stephenson the engineer of the 25 mile line in 1821. Stephenson built *Locomotion No. 1* to work on the line. The railway made a good profit by charging for the carriage of goods.

Stephenson fixed the width of the rails at 4 feet 8¹/₂ inches. He decided on this figure after measuring hundreds of

> ### KEY IDEAS
> - They built lines and locomotives
> - They used different gauges
> - They overcame physical obstacles

SOURCE 2
The opening of the Stockton and Darlington Railway, 1825.
▼

SOURCE 3

Nicholas Wood, a good friend of George Stephenson, wrote about the Stockton and Darlington railway:

On the level, or nearly level gradients, horses or locomotives are proposed. In ascending gradients, where the hills are too steep for the use of horses or locomotives, fixed engines and ropes should be adopted. In descending gradients, the use of self-acting planes (where the waggons rolled along the track using their own momentum) should be adopted.

colliery waggons, and taking the average distance between their wheels. Passengers were allowed to travel on the line but they had to have their own road carriages fastened onto a waggon. This is where the term railway-*carriage* comes from.

There was a lot of suspicion about **locomotives**. People were afraid that livestock would be frightened, and woodlands set on fire by sparks from the locomotive. Many believed that speeds of up to 12 mph were dangerous to the human body.

The Liverpool and Manchester Railway

The Bridgewater Canal had been hailed as a success when it was opened in 1767, but by the 1820s the link was considered to be inadequate for the rapidly developing industrial town of Manchester. The canal company which held a monopoly on links between Liverpool and Manchester, charged heavy tolls. Journeys were also slow. It was claimed that raw cotton took as long to get from Liverpool to Manchester as it did to get from America to Liverpool. Inspired by the success of the Stockton and Darlington line, a group of businessmen decided to build a railway from Liverpool to Manchester. George Stephenson was appointed chief engineer with his son Robert, as chief surveyor. The line attracted a lot of opposition from groups who felt their interests would suffer:

● Canal and turnpike trust owners feared a loss of trade and therefore profits.
● Local landowners objected to losing good farming land.

Despite this opposition an Act of Parliament, supported by William Huskisson MP, was granted to build the 35 mile stretch of double track line. The builders faced a number of obstacles:
● **Olive Mount**, near Liverpool – a deep **cutting** had to be made into it (Source 4).

SOURCE 4 ▲
A drawing of Olive Mount cutting.

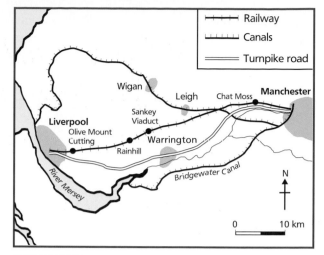

SOURCE 5 ▲
The route of the Liverpool and Manchester Railway.

● **Edgehill** – a long **tunnel** was constructed at Edgehill.
● **The River Sankey,** near Warrington – crossed by a long **viaduct.**
● **Chat Moss**, a huge peat bog, near Manchester – a firm **foundation** for the line was made by tipping in brushwood.
● **Protesters** who made their job difficult – surveyors **worked at night**.

Stephenson persuaded the directors of the company that locomotives should be used to pull the coaches and waggons. To choose the locomotive design that would be used, a competition – the **Rainhill Trials** – was held in 1829 with a prize of £500 offered to the winning engineer. The trials were held on a straight stretch of track at Rainhill, just outside Liverpool. Four engines were entered, and the competition was won by the *Rocket*, the engine designed by George and Robert Stephenson. It reached speeds of almost 30 mph.

The opening of the Liverpool and Manchester Railway in September 1830 was a spectacular occasion. It was attended by about 50,000 people including the Prime Minister, the Duke of Wellington. Tragically, William Huskisson, the politician who had done most to promote the railway, was knocked down and killed by a locomotive during the opening ceremony.

The Liverpool and Manchester Railway was a great success. The Directors of the Company were amazed at the number of passengers and merchants who wanted to use the new line.

	Passengers	Goods (tons)	Coal (tons)
1831	445,000	43,000	11,000
1835	474,000	231,000	116,000

The table above shows the use of railways in the first five years. At first, more money was made from passengers than freight, but the amount of goods transported increased. In 1835 the railway began to carry livestock which had been brought to England from Ireland. Soon supplies of fresh fish and vegetables were being transported. Thanks to the railway, people could enjoy a healthier and more varied diet. Raw cotton imported from America was carried in bulk to manufacturers so reducing costs. With the competition from the railway services, the local canal and coach companies found themselves facing financial ruin.

Following the success of the Liverpool and Manchester railway, other lines were built to meet the local needs of different areas. In 1838 the first cross-country line, the London

SOURCE 6 ▲
A mixed train of freight and passengers on the Liverpool and Manchester Railway.

and Birmingham railway, was completed. This line was designed by Robert Stephenson. It was a difficult line to build – long tunnels, cuttings and embankments had to be made along the 112-mile route. Much of this work was done in soft soil. The greatest feat was the building of the Kilsby Tunnel which took $2^1/2$ years to complete.

SOURCE 7 ▼
George Stephenson.

SOURCE 8 ▼
Robert Stephenson.

George Stephenson (1781-1848)
- Born at Wylam, near Newcastle-upon-Tyne.
- One of six children, the son of a poorly-paid colliery engine fireman.
- He taught himself to read and write at night school.
- At Killingworth Colliery he was appointed engine-wright in 1812 at a salary of £100 per year.
- His first engine was called *Blucher* which he built in 1814. This worked on the six mile stretch of waggonway which connected the Killingworth pit with the River Tyne.
- In 1821 he was appointed surveyor of the Stockton and Darlington line at a salary of £300 per year.
- He built *Locomotion No. 1* for this railway.
- He introduced the standard gauge.
- He became engineer of the Liverpool and Manchester railway.
- Together with his son Robert, he designed the *Rocket* which won the Rainhill Trials.

Robert Stephenson (1803-1859)
- George Stephenson's only son born near Newcastle.
- Became an apprentice at Killingworth before going to study engineering at Edinburgh University.
- Spent three years in South Africa building railways.
- Surveyor of the Liverpool and Manchester Railway.
- Engineer of the London and Birmingham Railway.
- Built the Britannia Tubular Bridge over the Menai Straits which opened in 1850.

SOURCE 9 ▶
Map of early railway development.

Isambard Kingdom Brunel (1806-1859)

The Great Western Railway: A group of Bristol merchants began to worry that Manchester, with its rail link, would attract more trade than Bristol. In 1832, they discussed the possibility of a railway linking Bristol to London. In March 1833 they went further, making Isambard Kingdom Brunel chief engineer and asking parliamentary permission for the railway. This was, however, refused because of objections from the Kennet and Avon Canal Company, the London and Windsor Railway, and various landowners and stage-coach operators. Another attempt to get permission was made in 1835 and, with the support of George Stephenson, an Act was passed.

The new railway company was known as the Great Western Railway (GWR). In order to ensure that the passengers travelled in comfort and ease, Brunel designed a line without bends and steep gradients. He also fixed the width of his rails at 7 feet 1 inch claiming that this broad gauge would give passengers a smoother, faster ride and allow the GWR to use larger and quicker locomotives. The last link in the line, the two mile Box Tunnel, was finished in June 1841 and the whole line from London to Bristol was open. Brunel is also famous for the Royal Albert Bridge across the Tamar between Plymouth and Saltash (Source 10). This was completed in 1859 just before his death.

Robert Stephenson's Britannia tubular bridge over the Menai Strait

Darlington
Stockton (1825)
Liverpool (1830)
Manchester
Crewe
Birmingham
Rugby
New towns grew because of railways
Bristol
Swindon
LONDON
Box Tunnel

Royal Albert Bridge, Saltash (Brunel)

SOURCE 10
Royal Albert Bridge over the River Tamar from Plymouth to Saltash, built to carry the Great Western Railway into Cornwall. ▼

Questions

1. What can you learn from Source 2 about early railways?

2. Why did the opening of the early railways attract so many people?

3. The scenes from the early railways are often drawings. Does this mean they are of little use to a historian trying to recreate the past?

4. Why were some people concerned about the use of locomotives on the early railways?

5. Why, and in what ways, did people object to the building of the early railways?

6. How did the merchants of Manchester benefit from the building of the Liverpool and Manchester Railway?

7. Was George Stephenson more important than any other person to the development of the railway system?

10.3 How difficult was it for the railway system to grow?

Public reaction

Landowners and farmers objected to the noise and the smell saying that the engines would set fire to crops, frighten cattle, stop hens laying and scare away game. Really what they feared was the value of their land falling. **Canal, turnpike and stage-coach owners** feared a loss of income. There were people who thought that the human body would not stand the speed of travel. People would be suffocated in the tunnels and ladies could be attacked in the carriages. Some **town officials** did not want the railways in their town.

Construction costs

The high cost of railway construction was due to:
- the cost of buying land;
- the cost of building lines over difficult ground;
- expensive tunnels, cuttings and viaducts to avoid steep gradients.

Providing a special labour force

All railway cuttings and embankments, tunnels and bridges had to be built by hand. The workers were called **navvies**. They were very strong and hard working. They were able to earn high wages, but their safety was ignored. They earned a reputation of being fierce, strong, big eaters, drinkers and fighters.

The battle of the gauges

Lines were at first built to two incompatible gauges, those of Stephenson and Brunel. This caused problems. It was settled by the **Gauge Regulating Act** of 1846 which made Stephenson's gauge of 4 feet 8^1/$_2$ inches the standard gauge. It was chosen as there were more lines in existence using this width of track. Brunel was disgusted that Stephenson's 'horse and cart' gauge had been chosen. The last broad gauge lines did not disappear until 1892 (see Source 13).

(see Source 13)

KEY IDEAS

- Builders faced problems
- Railways were privately financed
- The Government slowly became interested
- Rail travel gradually improved

SOURCE 11
Building the Tring cutting on the London and Birmingham Line, 1837. ▼

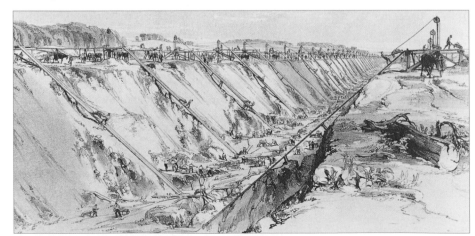

SOURCE 12

The battle between the rival gauges raged for almost thirty years so that at Gloucester through-passengers and goods had to change trains among the confusion of shouting out addresses of goods, the throwing of packages from track to track, the enquiries for missing articles, the loading, unloading and reloading.

A local history book, 1972

'Railway mania'

During the 1840s the pace of railway development increased. Many new lines were opened and the first major railway companies, like the Midland (1844) and the North Western (1846), were the result of the amalgamation of smaller lines. Almost every main town could be reached by rail.

The money for this amazing railway building programme was all invested by the public, much of it during the railway mania years of 1844 to 1848. This boom in railway share buying and speculation was similar to the canal mania of the 1790s. One of the leading figures in this boom was **George Hudson**, the 'railway king'. Hudson organised amalgamations and handled railway shares worth millions of pounds. In 1847 the railway 'bubble' burst. Many companies were found to be badly organised or phoney. Hudson's deception was found out and in 1849 he was disgraced.

However by 1870, there were 13,600 miles of railway. Road transport could not compete with the railways and many railway companies were very profitable.

Government control

Although the railways were privately funded, by the early 1840s Parliament felt that regulation was required:
● 1840 – the Board of Trade was authorised to inspect all new railways prior to their opening.
● 1842 – the Board of Trade was required to

hold official enquiries into railway accidents.
● The **Railway Act of 1844** made all companies run at least one train a day with fares of no more that one penny a mile and third class carriages with seats and roofs. The train was required to stop at all stations. (Even on these 'Parliamentary' trains travel was still expensive, and many railway companies ran them during the night.)
● The Gauge Regulating Act of 1846 introduced the standard gauge.

Changes and improvements

Improvements in comfort included the introduction of steam heating, gas lighting in carriages, restaurant cars, corridor trains, lavatories, sleeping carriages and windows in third-class carriages.

In the late 19th century, the overall length of track increased with the addition of local and branch lines. Steel rails replaced iron ones and in 1892, the Great Western railway stopped using the broad gauge track. Safety was improved with the introduction of standardised signalling and automatic brakes.

SOURCE 13 ▲
Navvies at work in 1892 on the GWR, replacing the broad-gauge rails.

uestions

1. Describe the difficulties faced by the builders of the early railways.

2. How successful was the Railway Act of 1844 in improving rail travel?

3. Did Government intervention make railway travel better?

10.4 *What was the impact of railways*

SOURCE 14
From Charles Dickens', Dombey and Son, written in 1848: ▼

> I left Dullborough in the days when there were no rail roads in the land; I left in a stage-coach. I was shunted back the other day by train and the first discovery I made was that the station had swallowed up the playing field. It was gone. The two beautiful hawthorn trees, the hedges the turf and all those buttercups and daisies had given place to stony roads; while beyond the station an ugly dark monster of a tunnel kept its jaw open as if it had swallowed them and was greedy for more destruction.

By 1850 the railway system had 7,500 miles of track in use and, despite objections, railways continued to spread reaching 21,429 miles by 1897. The coming of the railways was of enormous importance. They provided industry with a means of transport far superior to anything that had existed before, and encouraged tremendous economic growth. They were also a valuable source of employment. By encouraging people to travel, the railways brought about a social revolution.

Effects on industry: There was a huge demand for iron to be used for the rails, engines, trucks and buildings. It was estimated that rails alone took 15% of all iron output in the 1840s. The building industry grew with the increase in the need for bricks. The railways used up to about a third of the bricks produced. Timber was used in great quantities for sleepers, and in trucks, carriages and buildings. Mine owners no longer had to rely on the slow canals. They were now able to send more coal to the towns for industrial and domestic use. Railways themselves consumed large quantities of coal.

GROWTH OF THE RAILWAYS

Effects on jobs: Not only did the railways increase employment in the industries mentioned above, they also created jobs as signalmen, firemen, guards, drivers, booking clerks and station masters.

Effects on food: Fresh milk was carried overnight from the West Country to London. Fresh fish could be brought from the ports of Fleetwood, Grimsby and Lowestoft to the markets. Other fresh food such as dairy products, fresh vegetables and fruit could be sold in the cities and towns in good condition. This helped to increase the range and choice in the shops, and helped to improve the health of the nation. At the same time fertilizers, seed and machines could be brought to the farmers.

SOURCE 15 *Figures showing growth of railways.* ▶

Date	Miles of track	Passengers
1842	1,855	18,000
1847	3,942	51,000
1852	7,330	89,000
1857	9,092	139,000
1862	11,541	180,000
1867	14,235	288,000
1872	15,801	423,000
1877	17,074	549,000
1882	17,063	655,000
1887	19,574	734,000
1892	20,321	864,000
1897	21,429	1,103,000

TRADE AND INDUSTRY

SOURCE 16
From the Railway News, *1864:*

In the grey mists of the morning, we see a large portion of the supply of the great London markets rapidly unloaded from night trains: fish, Aylesbury butter and dairy-fed pork, apples, cabbages and cucumbers. Elsewhere in the country trains carried Manchester cotton goods, Liverpool cotton, Birmingham hardware, Staffordshire pottery and coal from Newcastle.

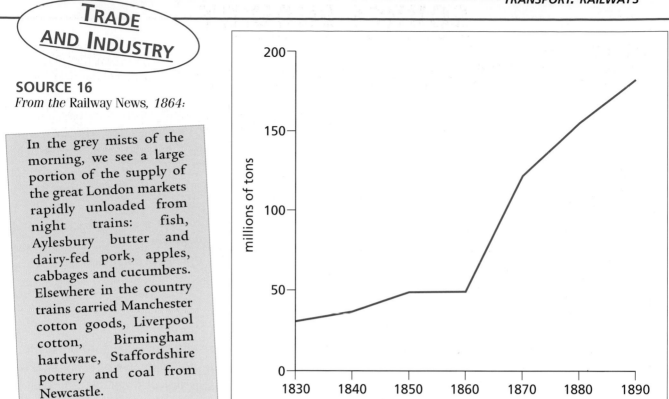

SOURCE 17 ▲
Coal production 1830-1890.

Effects on other forms of transport: The Turnpike Trusts suffered badly from the competition created by the railways as their income dropped despite attempts to raise their charges. The stage-coach companies also started to cut their charges, but they could not match the speed of the railways and resorted to carrying people short journeys to and from the railway stations. Canals actually remained cheaper than railways for goods traffic, and some canals continued to operate until late into the century – although by that time they had usually given up their long distance traffic. Even by 1850, the Bridgewater Canal was still carrying two-thirds of Manchester's goods. Some railway companies were frightened of canal competition. They bought out the canal companies, put up their charges to deter customers, and so put them out of business.

SOURCE 18 ▶
Pig iron production 1820-1860.

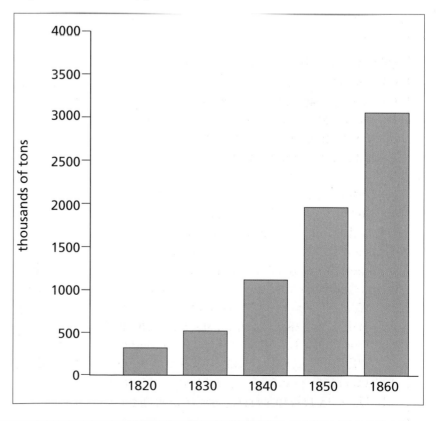

Effects on the landscape: Bridges, tunnels, embankments and cuttings altered the appearance of the countryside and railway towns grew up at Doncaster, Crewe and Swindon. Before the railways, most people had to live within walking distance of their jobs. As the century progressed, working-class suburbs sprang up. Better-off people moved further away from their place of work to live, and travelled to the towns by train. Several lines offered cheap workmen's return tickets. House-building materials were brought into the towns by railways thus making housing cheaper.

Excursions, holidays and leisure: From the early days special trains ran at reduced prices. Thomas Cook offered his first excursion ticket in 1841 from Leicester to Loughborough. The Great Exhibition in London encouraged family outings, and all the main companies offered cheap tickets.

SOURCE 19
From an article on the Social Effects of Railways, Chambers Journal, *1844:* ▼

Not the least effect of the railways is the opportunities that have been given to the humbler classes for recreation. Short trips give the working classes the chance to see what they would never have been able to see in the times of the old stage-coach. The worker cooped up and constantly breathing bad air, now has the opportunity on every available holiday, of making excursions into the country. A railway train takes masses of people of all levels of society. The rich are brought into contact with the poor and can talk to them. Nothing opens men's minds so much as seeing a variety of places and people.

As leisure time increased so holidays lengthened, and railways offered trips to the seaside. Seaside resorts such as Blackpool, Scarborough and Brighton as well as many others benefited and grew because of the railways. Towards the end of the century, sport became more organised with national leagues.

SOURCE 20
A painting of the arrival of the working men's train. ▼

SOURCE 21
From a book written in 1987: ▼

Passenger fares in the early days were far from cheap. It cost 10 shillings to travel first class from Birmingham to Derby and 30 shillings to London, and the Parliamentary train ran at inconvenient times. It was mainly the upper and middle classes who used the passenger services.

THE CLASS DIFFERENCE

Ending of local isolation: Trade unions and political parties grew in the late 19th century because they were able to organise national campaigns. Speakers, organisers and pamphlets could be sent rapidly all over the country. One of the major changes brought was the standardisation of time by using **Greenwich Mean Time** across the country so that trains could run to a timetable. National newspapers could now be printed in London and sent all over the country with everyone able to read the same stories. Letters could be sent at speed from one end of the country to the other. Police and troops could be moved quickly to maintain law and order. Railways made a wider choice of school possible, with many children travelling to public and boarding schools.

Questions

1. How were each of the following affected by the growth of railways?
   (a) The owner of a stage-coach business between London and Bristol;
   (b) A dairy farmer in the west country;
   (c) A shareholder in a canal company;
   (d) A person living in the town of Crewe;
   (e) A middle class family.

2. What does Source 20 tell you about the use of railways?

3. Does Source 21 agree with Source 22 about the use of railways?

4. Why do Sources 20 and 21 differ?

5. Explain the link between Sources 17 and 18, and railway development.

6. How useful is Source 14 to a historian studying the changes brought by the building of the railways?

7. How reliable is the view expressed in Source 19?

8. Do Sources 15 and 16 fully explain the decline of road and canal transport?

9. The development of railways was of more benefit to social life than to agriculture or industry. Do you agree?

◀ **SOURCE 22**
A third-class carriage on a 'Parliamentary' train.

103

11 TOWNS & PUBLIC HEALTH

11.1 *What was the condition of Britain's towns in the early 1800s* **?**

In Britain's rapidly growing towns and cities people were living in miserable squalor. In 1832, a Manchester doctor called Kay-Shuttleworth reported on part of the city called 'Little Ireland'. It was, he wrote, ideal for the outbreak of disease. The privies (very basic toilets) were difficult to reach because they were surrounded by filth. There were only two for every 250 people. Cellars measuring only 10 ft square were **overcrowded** with as many as ten people living in them. A weaver who lived in one of these cellars had to mop his floor every morning because of the water which drained into it.

Slums like these could be found elsewhere in Britain. Charles Dickens wrote about them in his novels, such as *Bleak House*, describing them as 'dumb, wet, silent horrors'. Houses could not be built fast enough to cope with the thousands of people from the countryside arriving at the factory gates for work. With no building rules and no one to ensure proper drainage or clean water supplies, closely packed 'back-to-back' houses were built by jerry builders at enormous speed.

Back-to-backs meant that the back wall of one house was shared with the house facing the other way on to the next street. This meant no back yards, nowhere to leave rubbish, and **no clean water supply**. Tenements were built several storeys high, so that landlords could cram as many people in as possible. The materials used were cheap and of poor quality: it was not long before walls were crumbling and damp. Sometimes a toilet would be provided over a cesspool or ash pit. If these were not cleaned out regularly, they would overflow. Where no toilets were provided, the human waste used to be thrown in the streets. 'Night-soilmen' were used in many towns to shovel the heaps of waste into carts and sell it to local farmers for manure.

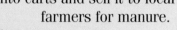

◀ **SOURCE 1**
A 19th-century picture of a typical city scene in Lambeth, south London.

Where drains existed, they were just open ditches, cleaned every few years by teams of 'scavengers'. With a water pump nearby, there was always the danger of contamination of the drinking water.

Hazards to health at work and in food

People suffered some of the worst **working conditions** in mines and factories. Bronchitis and asthma were caused by dust, while fumes from chemical processes, such as bleaching cloth (where chlorine is used) were dangerous because no attempts were made in the early 19th century to protect workers. Chimneys poured out soot and choking fumes, which everyone had to breathe.

Even **food** wasn't safe to eat. An enquiry in 1850 discovered that ground limestone was being added to flour, and sawdust to coffee. Bone-shavings found their way into beer, while goods such as sugar were often filthy.

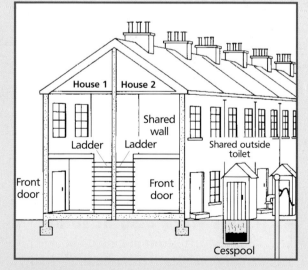

SOURCE 2 ▲
Diagram of back-to-back houses.

Why were death rates in the towns so high?

On average, how long might those in towns in the early 19th century be expected to live? In 1842 a survey in Manchester found that over half of the babies born never reached the age of 5. The average ages of death were:

- 17 years of age for a labourer;
- 20 years of age for a tradesman;
- 38 years of age for a middle-class professional.

Even so, awareness of such conditions only spread slowly. Death rates in the cities continued to be high. Why?

The population of Britain was increasing rapidly

It doubled in 50 years:

- in 1801 the population was 10.5 million;
- in 1851 it was 21 million.
  Then it doubled again:
- in 1901 it was 42 million.

Now look at the figures for the growth of towns and cities, called **urbanisation:**

- in 1800, only 25% of the population lived in towns;
- by 1901, 75% of the population lived in towns.

Britain became a country of town dwellers in an astonishingly short space of time.

Attitudes were also at fault

The 19th century is often called the age of '**laissez-faire**', or 'leave things alone'. Many believed that things would work out for the best if they were left alone. Government interference would only make things worse. In addition, it was argued that Government had no rights to interfere in what landlords did with their private property.

> **KEY IDEAS**
>
> Little was done to remove health risks because of:
>
> - 'laissez-faire' attitudes
> - no effective local government
> - little understanding of spread of disease

SOURCE 3
Punch *cartoon, 1849. A city alderman is admiring his reflection in the dirty canal of his industrial city.*
▼

The attitudes of richer people towards the poor was based on ignorance and fear. They rarely saw the slums, and thought that the people who lived there must be drunken, lazy and criminal. If they did not improve their own conditions it was their own fault, and nobody else's.

As for the poor, they had come to expect what one doctor, Southwood Smith, called the 'unhumanising' effects of filthy housing. And conditions in the countryside were often just as unpleasant as those in the towns.

There was little understanding of what caused disease

Medical science had not yet discovered that germs cause disease – Louis Pasteur did that in 1864.

However, it was known that there was a link between dirt and disease, but doctors were unsure how diseases were spread. As a result, treatments rarely worked. Doctors tried smoke, by burning tar and vinegar in infected houses, or ice-cold baths, or the old traditional method of applying leeches to suck the 'poisoned' blood out of the body. Hospitals were little help. They had a reputation for unhygenic wards, untrained staff and refusing to admit patients with infectious diseases in case they spread.

Before 1835 there was no single system of local government

Towns had their own rules and regulations, but often no way of carrying them out properly. There were numerous water companies, and separate committees to look after sewerage, street lighting and street cleaning. It was confusing and chaotic.

Older towns with unelected councils looked after themselves.

Where councils were elected, those who voted for them were rate payers. Rates were a local tax paid to the local authority by those owning property. Rate payers did not want to pay more than they had to, and expected councillors not to start ambitious schemes to clear slums, pave streets or build drains.

State benevolence [help] is a melancholy system which tends to reduce a large mass of the people to the condition of the nursery, where the children look to the father and mother and do nothing for themselves.

Lord Shaftesbury, a noted reformer of factory and living conditions.

Questions

Here is a list of reasons why public health problems were so serious in 19th-century towns:

- *industrialisation*
- *the rapid growth of towns*
- *attitudes to government action*
- *chaotic local government*
- *lack of medical knowledge*

1. *Explain which of these reasons had been present before 19th-century urban problems became so severe.*

2. *Which of these reasons arose at the end of the 18th and start of the 19th centuries?*

3. *Explain how all these reasons played their part in creating such serious and long-lasting problems.*

4. *Explain why Source 3 is a biased view of the need for public health reform.*

11.3 Why was cholera such a threat to public health?

William Sproat, a seaman in Sunderland, was struck down in October 1831 with vomiting, diarrhoea and fever. His skin turned a blueish-purple colour and he died. His death was the first to be recorded in the town from a painful and horrifying disease – cholera.

The disease had arrived on a ship that came into the port. People were terrified by how quickly cholera spread and how little doctors could do about it. It struck at middle class people, not just slum dwellers, making the threat from this 'new' disease seem so much worse. In 1831, 13,000 people died in three months alone, and there were four more cholera epidemics during the century.

SOURCE 6 ▼
A Rotherham local Board of Health reported:

In Millgate there are foul piggeries, large piles of filth, no drainage and no pavement. The houses stand one above the other on a steep hill, so that the refuse from one house finds its way through the walls of the one below. One tenant said, 'A privy runs into the well when it has rained, so we must get water where we can'.

The privies on Mr Ward's property and the liquid from the piggeries drain down and under the cottages belonging to Mrs Holland. Mr John Needham's property has two privies less than six feet from the houses and the bedroom looks into open cesspools. Tenants complained the stench was as strong in the bedrooms as in the privies themselves.

BEFORE THE CHOLERA

SOURCE 7 ▼
Piggeries in Exeter's streets.

Doctors advised that water should be boiled and 'if there be offensive smells from cesspools, complain to your landlord'. But doctors could not agree about how cholera was spread. Some thought it was by touch. Others thought it was carried by smells, or 'miasmas'. They had few answers.

A doctor said that the disease could be avoided if people had 'good habits', because, he claimed, 'drunkenness and late hours are great friends of the cholera'.

In fact, the cholera bacteria was not discovered until 1883. But in 1854 Dr John Snow found a link between polluted water and the disease. He investigated 500 deaths near to a water pump in Broad Street, London. Once Dr Snow had ordered the removal of the pump handle, no new cases of cholera were reported.

DENYING THE PROBLEM

SOURCE 8

The Government closed the port of Sunderland. In response, a public meeting of shipowners and merchants declared: ▼

It is the opinion of this meeting, based on Parish Inspectors, that this town is now in a more healthy state than is usual for this time of year. We have enquired about the disorder which has caused panic throughout the kingdom and we have found it not Indian cholera. The few deaths from sickness have been caused by common bowel complaints. The paragraph put in the London papers stating that Indian cholera was brought to Sunderland on a ship is a wicked lie. No seamen or Customs Officer has made such a complaint. The action by the government in guarding the port with a warship is totally uncalled for.

Questions

1. What do these sources tell you about the best ways to avoid catching cholera?

2. What does Source 6 tell you about what conditions in Rotherham were really like?

3. How reliable is Source 8 to a historian studying the outbreak cholera in 1831 in Sunderland?

4. How useful is Source 9 to a historian studying what people thought about cholera?

5. 'A written source like Source 6 is more accurate than a drawing (Source 7), because it will contain more factual information'. Do you agree?

THE EPIDEMIC SPREADS

SOURCE 9

In three months the cholera epidemic had reached London. In 1832. Mrs Nicholls, who lived near London, wrote to a friend: ▼

My dear Charlotte,
The cholera is a great source of worry at present. It is a most awful visit by the disease. Most medical men say it is infectious, its having appeared in London. Its progress is slow and alarming, yet I hope those of good habits have not much to fear at present. We know now what hot weather may produce. There has been a Board of Health here for some time and several gentlemen discuss the best precautions to be taken in case cholera appears. I should be glad to hear how you all are in health at this eventful period.
With sincere regards,
S. Nicholls

SOURCE 10 ▶

Posters and broadsheets advised people how to prevent cholera:

HOW TO AVOID THE CHOLERA!
PLAIN DIRECTIONS FOR POOR PEOPLE

Whatever may be the cause of Cholera, this is certain, that hitherto almost without exception this pestilence has been the portion of the poor, and we know that those who are in want of food and clothing most quickly fall the victims of this disease. Let therefore the working man, the head of a family reflect that by laziness or drunkenness, he not only exposes himself, but in all probability his wife and children to the attacks of Cholera, by depriving them of the comforts and necessaries of life.

Cleanse out and thoroughly scour your water-butts and cisterns; boil the water before you drink it. Impure water is the cause of many diseases.

Should the Cholera, however, attack you, or any in your house, don't be alarmed – it is not catching – the disease is now better understood than heretofore; mild cases are really cured, and the worst cases are not always fatal.

Two of these pills should be taken at once, with a tablespoonful of brandy, and one pill every half hour. But don't delay getting a doctor.

Cayenne pepper	12 grains
Opium	6 grains
Oil of cloves	6 drops

Aromatic confection sufficient to make into twelve pills

Brandy is certainly most valuable in Cholera to those who have not been in the habit of spirits drinking; those who have constantly taken it, derive little or no good from it.

11.4 *Why did the health of the towns improve so slowly?*

A series of reports in the 1830s and 1840s captured the attention of the well-off who, before, had known almost nothing about the miserable squalor of the slums. As one historian put it, people now began to 'realise that they were living on a dungheap'.

Edwin Chadwick (1800-90) had been Secretary to the Poor Law Commissioners from 1834, and he had seen that disease caused poverty. This concerned him, because paupers were given relief from the Poor Rate which was a public expense (see pages 128-129). In 1842 he produced his best-selling *Report on the Sanitary Conditions of the Labouring Population of Great Britain*. This horrified its readers.

At around the same time, the collection of proper statistics for births and deaths began. This showed that the death rates were high. However, change was slow to come – even though there was another serious cholera outbreak in 1844.

KEY IDEAS

- In 1848 a Public Health Act set up some local Boards of Health

- Boards could not force improvements in sanitation

- People opposed the way the Government interfered in public health

- Chadwick's Board of Health was brought to an end in 1854

SOURCE 11

Dr Southwood Smith gave this evidence to the 1844 Royal Commission:

The evil will continue so long as our cities contain so many filthy lanes, so long as the houses there are little better than hovels, so long as dunghills are nearby.

Why, then, should we not have a law that would clear these hovels to the ground – that would regulate the width of every street – that would control the ventilation of every house?

SOURCE 12 ▲
This cartoon in Punch *(1849) attacks the lack of interest in misery and squalor.*

The 'Dirty Party'

Many people in the 19th century held 'laissez-faire' attitudes. They said that Parliament had no right to force property owners to clear heaps of refuse or clear filthy piggeries from courtyards. They thought that, if people lived in squalor, it was their own fault and no one else's.

Public Health Act 1848 – a very small step

It was not until 1848 that a Public Health Act was passed. It set up a **General Board of Health** in London. Chadwick became one of its commissioners. The Board

could create **local Boards of Health:**
- if 10% of the local population asked for one, or,
- if the death rate in an area was above 23 per 1,000 people.

Local Boards could control water supplies, cemeteries, sewerage, the paving of streets and their drainage.

The Act made little difference, because the Boards could not force towns to improve conditions. For example, Manchester did not choose to have a Medical Officer of Health until 1868. Only one-sixth of the population was covered by local Boards of Health, when the General Board of Health was closed down in 1854. Many slum dwellers still had no sink or water supply in their homes. Even if a house had a water supply it had to be paid for, so sometimes the supply was turned off because of the cost. Open sewers still ran down the street.

There were, however, local examples of progress. Sir John Simon was Medical Officer of Health for London (1848-55). He proved that death rates could be lowered if the water

SOURCE 13

No. 2 Wild Court – slum housing. ▲

supply was clean and supplied through pipes, instead of coming straight from the polluted River Thames. He insisted that rubbish was collected from the streets and the cesspools drained. By 1865, London's sewage was channelled away from the city. Other cities followed this example. Cholera deaths were reduced, even though 20,000 died of it in 1865-1866.

Reform was slow to come:
- A **Sanitary Act** in 1868 forced local authorities to appoint sanitary inspectors.
- In 1871 the **Local Government Board** was set up to oversee all local public health services.

The Public Health Act 1875 – a major step forward

- Every area had to have a Medical Officer of Health and a sanitary inspector.
- Councils were given powers to build sewers, drains, and public toilets.
- Councils had to make sure that refuse was collected, and the water supply was controlled.
- Local authorities could disinfect houses if someone had caught an infectious disease.

Even more could be done when County Councils (1888) and District Councils (1894) were set up.

SOURCE 14

This appeared in The Times, *August 1854, the day after it had been decided that Chadwick's Board of Health should be disbanded:*

We prefer to take our chance of cholera and the rest than be bullied into health. There is nothing a man so hates as being cleaned against his will, or having his floors swept, his walls whitewashed, his pet dungheaps cleared away, or his thatch forced to give way to slate ... It is a positive fact that many have died of a good washing ... Not so thought Mr Chadwick, and he set to work. Master John Bull was scrubbed, and rubbed, and small-toothcombed, till the tears came into his eyes and his teeth chattered ...

Questions

1. Why was the 1848 Public Health Act important?

2. Why did some people oppose Chadwick?

3. Which sources support laissez-faire and which sources support the idea of more government action? Explain your answer.

4. Despite the evidence of terrible conditions in the towns, why do you think progress in public health was so slow?

5. Why was the 1875 Public Health Act important?

11.5 Were housing conditions improving in the 19th century?

What were the living conditions in the countryside?

In the 1860s and 1870s, cholera, tuberculosis and smallpox epidemics caused health scares in the towns – but was life any better in the countryside? The answer partly depends on how prosperous farming was at any particular time. Historians agree that agriculture (and therefore the agricultural workers) went through hard times at the beginning and end of the century, but experienced good times in between.

Sources 15 and 16, give different interpretations of life in the countryside. Source 16 is written by a historian who argues that country life was just as unhealthy as in the towns. Source 15, shows a romantic view of a comfortable and charming rural cottage. Many Victorian artists painted similar pictures because they could sell their paintings to rich townspeople who wanted to look back to what they thought was a golden age before the days of ugly machinery and slums.

SOURCE 16

There were rural slums just as bad as the rookeries of London. Decaying thatched roofs are neither wind- nor rain-proof and make a first class home for vermin. Because the cottages had neither ceiling nor flooring, the droppings from the roofs fell straight on the inhabitants and their bits of furnishings, and added to the muddy filth underfoot. Fowls roosted in the rafters and pigsties were just under the window. Cottages built to house one family were inhabited by up to 36 persons at a time. The agricultural labourer was miserably housed.

Written in 1974 by Enid Gauldie, an expert on working class housing.

KEY IDEAS

- Housing conditions in the countryside were often as bad as in the cities
- Housing Acts only slowly forced landlords to improve the slums
- Private individuals such as Cadbury and Chamberlain only made a small impact

SOURCE 15
A painting by Maurice Harvey, a late 20th century American artist who specialises in rural scenes of this type. ▼

Which source gives the more accurate interpretation of country life? This depends on the motives of the writer or artist, and on what information they have used to arrive at their interpretation.

How far did housing improve during the 19th century?

Twenty-seven housing laws were passed in the second half of the 19th century. These included:

- **The Housing (Torrens) Act (1868).** This said that landlords had to keep property in good repair. If repairs were not carried out, the local authority could (but did not have to) force the landlord to make the houses good.

SOURCE 17

In 1873, the Hertfordshire Mercury *newspaper pointed out that Dr Ogle, Medical Officer of Health, had reported on:*

the filthy and overcrowded conditions of some labourers' cottages. Eleven persons were in the habit of sleeping in the bedroom of one of these cottages and besides being thus overcrowded, it was so much in ruins as to be entirely unfit for human habitation. As might be expected Dr Ogle traces deaths to the foul and poisonous air inhaled by the occupants of these terribly crowded cottages.

● **The Artisans' Dwellings Act 1875.** This gave local authorities more power to clear areas of bad housing, and to pay landlords compensation if their houses were pulled down. Rules were included about the size of rooms, the spaces between buildings and standards of sanitation.

● **The Housing of the Working Classes Act (1890).** This said that local authorities could demolish slums and build '**council houses**'.

The Government was now taking some action. However, progress in housing conditions was still very slow. This was because:

● Local authorities did not like asking ratepayers to pay towards better housing for the poor.

● The Government did not provide money for building 'council houses'.

● When slums were pulled down, few were replaced – so there was more overcrowding.

● Back-to-back houses continued to be built up to 1909.

Some **individuals** tried to improve housing conditions. **Octavia Hill** bought and repaired slums in London. Her tenants were taught the importance of cleaning and 'good habits'.

George Cadbury (the chocolate manufacturer) built the 'model village' of Bournville for his workers. The houses had gardens, there were leisure facilities and a village green with shops. Children brought up there were taller on average than those in Birmingham's slums.

Another manufacturer, **William Hesketh Lever** (the soap maker) also built a 'model village', Port Sunlight, on Merseyside for his workers. However, these 'model' villages made little difference to housing shortages.

Joseph Chamberlain, Mayor of Birmingham, led one of the **councils** which did make an impact on slums. Birmingham City Council bought 40 acres of factories and houses in the city centre which they demolished. (The factories were moved to the suburbs.) Private builders then put up rows and rows of decent – if dull – houses. Although housing conditions were better, the rents for these new houses were still too high for poor families.

Questions

1. Does Source 15 or Source 16 give a more accurate interpretation of rural life? Use what you know about 19th century public health to answer the question.

2. Why do some artists and authors still hold a romantic view of 19th-century country life?

3. Why is it difficult to decide what conditions were really like in a Victorian village?

4. What new housing was provided for the working class? Why was some of it called 'model housing'?

5. Study these factors:
   ● the actions of individuals;
   ● the actions of local councils;
   ● Government Housing Acts.
   How far did all these factors link together to bring about real improvements in working class housing up to 1900?

6. Only slow progress was made towards providing decent housing for the poor in the 19th century. Why is this difficult to explain?

MEDICINE

12.1 *What progress was being made in medicine during the 18th century* **?**

SOURCE 1
The cowpock – or the wonderful effects of the new inoculation, *a cartoon drawn by Gillray for the Anti-Vaccinarian Society in 1802.*

THIS SECTION ANSWERS:

12.1 *What progress was being made in medicine during the 18th century?*

12.2 *How successful were the attempts to deal with disease, pain and infection in the 19th century?*

12.3 *What led to the 20th century revolution in antibiotics?*

12.4 *A health revolution – health for all?*

12.5 *What are the major threats to health at the end of the 20th century?*

At the beginning of the 18th century, medical knowledge was limited. The main groups of medical professionals were:
● physicians;
● surgeons;
● apothecaries.

Physicians were 'gentlemanly'. They had usually studied at a university, charged high fees, and were full of their own importance. The College of Physicians acted as an exclusive club for its members instead of spreading and increasing medical knowledge. Physicians had no knowledge of the existence of germs.

Next in rank were the **surgeons**. They performed amputations, treated wounds, set bones, and bled patients (a common medical treatment). Originally they had been grouped together with barbers, but in 1745, the Company of Surgeons was formed to separate them. Because of their improved status, surgeons were allowed to dissect executed criminals (before, they had learnt about anatomy by secretly cutting up corpses bought from grave robbers). After 1750, some hospitals allowed student surgeons to follow a proper course of training. However, they did not have antiseptics or anaesthetics.

The **apothecary** (chemist) had the lowest status of the three. They were required to have a licence and made up prescriptions on the orders of physicians. Unlicensed (and so illegal) apothecaries would make up medicines for people who could not afford a doctor.

The very poor turned to women who knew herbal recipes for curing common ailments. These women also acted as **midwives**.

Did hospitals do more harm than good?

Hospitals provided little help to the sick:
- They were filthy and unhygienic.
- Hospitals did not treat patients with infectious diseases. These people had to stay at home where they risked infecting their families.
- Hospital nurses were untrained and badly paid. They had no medical knowledge.
- Bethlehem Hospital (known as Bedlam), the only public 'madhouse', allowed people in to look at the patients being treated. Treatment was brutal.
- Even by 1801 there were only about 3,000 hospital beds in England and Wales.

However, efforts were made to improve matters:
- Hospitals, such as Guys in London, were set up after 1720 by private charities.
- 'Lying-in' (maternity) hospitals were built. These provided some training for midwives (many of them men). However, poor hygiene meant high death rates.
- New lunatic asylums offered better treatment to the mentally ill.
- The first isolation hospital for infectious diseases was set up in 1801.

The fight against disease: smallpox

Smallpox is a highly infectious disease. In the 18th century death rates from the disease were alarmingly high. People who survived could be left blind, or at the very least scarred with pock-marks. In the 1720s, Lady Mary Wortley Montagu, helped introduce the idea of **inoculation** against smallpox to England from Turkey – pus from a smallpox sore was put into a small cut. If this brought on a mild case of smallpox it could provide immunity from a severe case of the disease. Unfortunately some people became seriously ill and died.

A Gloucestershire doctor, Edward Jenner, noticed that dairymaids who caught cowpox, a mild disease, rarely caught smallpox. He concluded that cowpox provided immunity from smallpox. In 1796, he experimented on eight-year-old James Phipps by taking pus from a cowpox sore and rubbing it into a cut on his arm. This **vaccination** (from the Latin word 'vacca', which means cow) gave the boy immunity – when he was later inoculated with smallpox it had no effect.

The 'Anti-Vaccinarian Society' criticised Jenner's work. Was it really safe? they asked. They feared people could be forced to be vaccinated. Despite this opposition, a series of acts were passed between 1853 and 1871 making vaccination compulsory. As a result smallpox was eventually conquered.

KEY IDEAS

- There was little understanding of disease
- Hospitals did more harm than good
- Medical education and training was in its infancy
- Jenner developed a vaccination against smallpox in 1796
- It took 100 years for vaccination to conquer smallpox

12.2 *How successful were the attempts to deal with disease, pain and infection in the 19th century* ?

Why was Pasteur so important?

Louis Pasteur made great advances in understanding where infection and disease came from. People had thought that germs just grew out of rotting vegetable or animal matter as a form of 'spontaneous generation'.

● His experiments showed that broth decayed only when it was exposed to the air. In that way he showed that it must be germs, carried in the air, that caused decay and disease.

● Pasteur published his germ theory of disease in 1861.

● He then grew microbes (the germs) of certain diseases in the laboratory which he injected in weak doses into animals. Antibodies were created in the blood providing protection (immunity) against stronger forms of disease.

● Pasteur's work resulted in vaccinations (immunisations) against cholera (1880), anthrax (a disease of sheep and cattle, 1881) and rabies (1895).

How did Robert Koch carry on Pasteur's work?

Robert Koch, a German doctor, attempted to find and recognise different microbes. He

SOURCE 2
Progress in dealing with disease, pain and infection.▼

KEY IDEAS

● Pasteur developed the germ theory of disease

● Simpson introduced chloroform as an anaesthetic

● Lister's carbolic spray helped reduce infection during surgery

● Florence Nightingale improved nursing standards

SOURCE 3 ▲
An operation using anaesthetic and carbolic sprays. However, although antiseptic is being used, the doctors are wearing their everyday clothes.

1847 Chloroform used as an anaesthetic	**1853** Compulsory smallpox vaccinations	**1855** Dr John Snow publishes evidence that cholera was a disease carried in the water supply	**1858** General Medical Council set up; registration of doctors begins	**1860** Nightingale Training School	**1864** Pasteur links airborne microbes to infection

developed a process of staining microbes so they could be seen clearly under a microscope and studied.

This work was the foundation for developing vaccinations to fight typhoid (1896), tetanus (1927), whooping cough (1952), polio (1954) and measles (1964).

Pain

Before there were anaesthetics, surgery could only be quick and uncomplicated to prevent causing the patients even more pain.
- Around 1800, Sir Humphrey Davy experimented with laughing gas (**nitrous oxide**) to stop toothache.
- Many years later, Robert Liston used **ether** to put a patient to sleep during an amputation. Ether, however, affected the lungs and caused coughing.
- In 1847 Dr James Simpson, Professor of Midwifery at Edinburgh University, used **chloroform** to help women through childbirth.

Despite this breakthrough, there was opposition to anaesthetics.
- Doctors worried that chloroform might kill patients.
- Religious objectors claimed that it was the will of God that humans suffer pain, especially during childbirth.

However, when Queen Victoria used chloroform in childbirth in 1857, many people overcame their worries. Longer, more complex surgery was now possible.

Infection

- Death rates from blood poisoning and gangrene after an operation could be as high as 90%.
- Dried old blood congealed on tables, instruments and surgeons' frock coats.

Sometimes one 'ward-sponge' would clean up septic wounds from several patients.
- In 1865, Joseph Lister, Professor of Surgery at Glasgow University, studied Pasteur's work. He successfully prevented the germs in the air invading wounds, by covering them with lint soaked in carbolic acid. The acid acted as an antiseptic. Lister went on to develop a carbolic acid pump which sprayed antiseptic onto a surgical patient (Source 3). Deaths from infection fell dramatically.

What impact did Florence Nightingale have in improving standards in hospitals?

Florence Nightingale was a tough and determined woman. She became a nurse at a time when many people thought that nursing was for women who were 'too weak, too drunken, too dirty or too bad to do anything else'. During the Crimean war, she was Superintendent of Nursing. She battled with army officers to get basic hygiene established, and clean dressings and better food provided in the military hospitals. This reduced death rates and made her famous.

On her return to Britain, money was raised to open the Nightingale School of Nursing at St. Thomas' Hospital in London. It opened in 1860 and, by 1907, just under 2,000 nurses had been trained. Nightingale had worked hard for a more professionally trained nursing staff for hospitals.

Questions

1. How did Florence Nightingale, James Simpson and Joseph Lister change the practice of medicine?

2. Why might the work of Pasteur and Koch be regarded as 'turning points' in the development of medicine?

1865	1870	1878	1880s	1890	1900
Antiseptic sprays used	Elizabeth Garrett Anderson qualifies as the first woman to be able to practice as a doctor in Britain	Identification of germs which caused septicaemia in wounds by Robert Koch; techniques developed for growing and isolating germs	Tuberculosis, typhoid, cholera and tetanus germs identified	Diphtheria vaccine first manufactured	Landsteiner identifies the four blood groups

12.3 *What led to the 20th-century revolution in antibiotics* ?

The drugs revolution

By 1900, vaccinations had been successfully used to fight smallpox and diphtheria. Later, vaccines would be developed to fight polio and tuberculosis. However, there were still many germs for which doctors had no cure.

Killing germs – finding the 'magic bullet'

Lister had shown how antiseptics killed germs outside the body. Now, scientists wanted something that could attack and destroy germs inside the body, for instance in the blood, without harming the patient. They wanted to find a 'magic bullet' to be 'fired' at a specific target (a disease).

- The German biologist Paul Ehrlich experimented with hundreds of chemicals that did not work.
- He found Salvarsan 606 in 1910 – it was the first **magic-bullet drug**.

Other 'magic bullets' were found in the 1930s.

- Scientist Gerhard Domagk experimented with the use of Prontosil, a red dye.
- He treated his daughter, who was dying from blood poisoning (septicaemia), with a massive dose of Prontosil, and she recovered.

Prontosil defeated the bacteria which caused septicaemia. It did this by stopping the bacteria developing and reproducing. The name given to the 'magic bullet' drugs was **Sulphonamides**. Very soon sulphonamide drugs were being used against pneumonia, scarlet fever and meningitis. Magic bullets were a tremendous breakthrough. However, something stronger was needed to deal with the powerful bacteria found in infected wounds.

KEY IDEAS

- 'Magic bullet' drugs went straight to the germs without damaging healthy tissue
- Alexander Fleming made the chance discovery of penicillin
- The Second World War made mass production of penicillin urgent

SOURCE 4
Penicillin mould on the dish on which it was discovered.

The story of penicillin: its discovery

During the First World War, Alexander Fleming had worked in the Army Medical Corps. He had seen the effects of deep wound infection caused by shrapnel, bullets, and the filthy conditions in the trenches. Many soldiers had died from blood poisoning and gangrene. After the war, Fleming became a research assistant at St Mary's hospital, London. He worked hard to look for a treatment for the bacteria (staphylococcus) which caused blood poisoning.

SOURCE 5

Fleming now tried to grow more of the mould and turn it into a pure drug.

Penicillin is an unstable substance. It very quickly goes off. At that time there were no chemical methods which could deal with such unstable substances. It was too soon. Chemistry had not progressed enough.

Fleming tried to get help from other laboratories but these failed. Many years later, Fleming said, 'I had failed for want of adequate chemical help'.

From Alexander Fleming and Penicillin, *by Howard Hughes, 1974.*

Fleming's discovery of penicillin was an accident. He used to grow germs on culture dishes, which he carelessly left lying around the laboratory. In 1928 he noticed that some mould had grown on a dish – as shown in Source 4. The mould had killed the germs around it. There was a clear area round the large white area of mould where the bacteria had been prevented from growing. That mould was penicillin, but when Fleming published his discovery it attracted little interest.

The story of penicillin: manufacturing the drug

The work of chemists: Fleming found it difficult to grow more penicillin, as Source 5 shows. Ten years later, at Oxford, Howard Florey and Ernst Chain (funded by the Government) took up his work. Chain succeeded in making a concentrated form of penicillin from the mould which was used successfully on mice.

The needs of wartime: During the Second World War the death rates for soldiers with deep wounds were alarmingly high. This made the development of penicillin more urgent. However, at the beginning of the war penicillin could not be mass produced. Mould had to be grown on thousands of milk bottles to produce a small quantity of the drug.

A human experiment: Penicillin was not tried out on a human patient until 1941. A policeman with a severe infection was treated with the drug, and he immediately improved.

Tragically, he died when supplies of the drug ran out. Fleming also tried out penicillin on an ill friend in 1942. Within a week of his first injection, the friend's recovery was almost complete.

Government help, and new technology: After America entered the Second World War, the US Government gave $80 million to drug companies to develop mass production of penicillin. It was eventually found that melons were suitable for growing large quantities of the mould. Technology then helped by creating huge fermentation tanks where growth took place. By 1944, sufficient penicillin was being made to save thousands of soldiers' lives.

Penicillin was the first **antibiotic** – it was seen as a miracle drug as it could tackle many different forms of bacteria. Since 1945 other antibiotics have been developed, such as streptomycin which is used to treat tuberculosis.

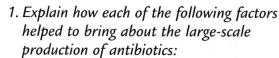

Questions

1. Explain how each of the following factors helped to bring about the large-scale production of antibiotics:

   (a) chance – the culture left on the dish;.
   (b) the role of individuals – Fleming, Florey and Chain;
   (c) warfare;
   (d) Government efforts;
   (e) technology and industry.

2. Which factor do you think was the most important? Explain your choice.

3. Why could these developments not have happened earlier than in the 20th century?

12.4 *A health revolution – health for all* ?

Why was the National Health Service introduced?

The struggle of the Second World War (1939-45) produced a new mood, which led to the formation of the National Health Service.

Before the war there was only a patchy system of health care:

- Doctors charged fees for their visits and for treatment.
- There were plenty of doctors in well-off districts, but not many in poor areas.
- Large numbers of people never received treatment because they could not afford it.
- Only half the population was covered by health insurance.
- Hospitals were run either by charities, which needed 'flag day' collections to keep them going, or by local authorities.
- There were not enough hospital beds.

During the war, however, people were willing to make sacrifices and pool what they had, for the benefit of everybody. There was a determination to improve social conditions and health. The effects of better health care and preventative medicine were seen during the war. For example, children were at great risk from diphtheria and, before the war, 3,000 a year died from it. After a free immunisation programme deaths fell to 818.

In 1942, William Beveridge produced his report into the welfare system. He said there were '*Five Giants on the road to progress: Want, Disease, Squalor, Ignorance and Idleness*'. Out of the mood of the country and the Beveridge report came the National Health Service (NHS).

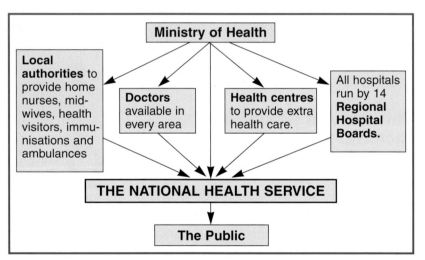

SOURCE 6
How the National Health Service worked. ▲

The first day of the NHS

The National Health Service covered every kind of medical service (Source 6 shows how the NHS was organised). The first day of free health care, called the '**Appointed Day**', was 5 July, 1948. Doctors' surgeries were overrun with patients.

- Over 8 million people who had not seen a doctor before swelled surgery lists.
- People asked for treatment for illnesses they would have ignored before because of the cost.

On Monday morning you will wake up in a new Britain, in a state which takes over its citizens six months before they are born, providing free care and services for their early years, their schooling, sickness, workless days, widowhood and retirement.

The Daily Mail, *July 1948.*

● Waiting lists for spectacles and dental treatment quickly grew long, because so many people had not been able to afford dentists and opticians before.

Many nurses liked the start of the NHS. After years of struggling along on the bare minimum they had plenty of medical supplies. They were amazed by all the cotton wool, clean bandages and medicines they had. The public also seemed enthusiastic.

The NHS was a remarkable achievement – but not everyone was happy.

to win the doctors over. They would be allowed some private 'pay' beds in hospitals. It had been a difficult process, but in the end 90% of doctors joined the NHS.

The NHS in difficulties

● The NHS was (and still is) costly. In 1948 the NHS cost £200 million – in 1975 it cost £5,200 million. At the start people rushed for treatment.

● Costs increased and there was criticism of the higher taxes which had to be paid because of the NHS.

● In 1951, charges for dentures, spectacles and prescriptions had to be introduced.

● There are more old people in Britain than before. They need more health care.

● Modern technology and surgery is expensive.

SOURCE 9
'Here he comes boys'. This cartoon of doctors trying to trip up Nye Bevan is from the Daily Mirror, *1946.* ▲

Why were some doctors against the National Health Service?

Nye Bevan (1897-1960), ex-miner and trade union official, and the Minister of Health and Housing in 1945, takes much of the credit for the formation of the NHS. His plain speaking angered many doctors, who thought they would end up working for the Government in a huge state system. They wanted to carry on privately treating paying patients. These doctors came close to ruining the new NHS. Two months before the 'Appointed Day', doctors were threatening a strike. Bevan managed to give in just enough

Bevan said in a speech to the House of Commons, April 1946:

A person ought not to be put off from seeking medical help at the earliest possible stage by the worry of doctor's bills. Our hospital organisation has grown up with no plan. In the older industrial districts, hospital facilities are inadequate.

Questions

1. Why was the National Health Service an improvement on what had gone before?

2. What problems did the NHS face (a) before it was set up, and (b) after it was set up?

3. Are sources 7 and 8 unreliable to a historian who is studying the start of the National Health Service?

4. Are cartoons useful sources about the introduction of the National Health Service?

12.5 *What are the major threats to health at the end of the 20th century* **?**

Has the health of the nation improved? The following factors have played their part in helping medicine to progress.

Medical technology

Screening and the diagnosis of patients have improved. Although X-rays developed from around 1895, the two World Wars showed how important they were in identifying soldiers' injuries. After 1945, mass X-ray units, many of them mobile, carried out large-scale screenings for diseases such as tuberculosis. Since then, technology has advanced: scanners produce images of cross-sections of the body; ultrasound uses sound waves to check on unborn babies; heart cardiographs measure heart signals; and fibre optics allow tiny cameras to be threaded inside the body from where they transmit pictures onto a screen.

In the 19th century no one understood why, sometimes, **blood transfusions** did not work. The breakthrough came in 1901 when different blood groups were discovered. Doctors then knew that patients had to have blood from the same group as their own. The demand for blood during the two World Wars resulted in blood donation becoming more organised – to ensure blood was available – and blood being separated out into plasma (the liquid) and red blood cells, so that it kept for longer.

Surgery

Anaesthetic is given by injection instead of taken by breathing it in. This is much safer, and the amount of anaesthetic given can be more tightly controlled.

Transplants have become more common –

KEY IDEAS

- Progress in technology, surgery, public health and the environment have improved health at the end of the 20th century

- Major threats to health still exist – heart disease, cancer, AIDS

- The costs of health care are increasing rapidly

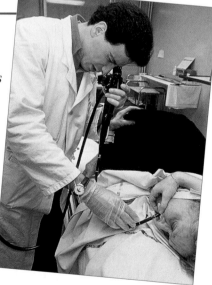

SOURCE 10
Fibre optics have let doctors see inside the body without major surgery.

▶

kidneys, liver, heart, lungs, bone marrow, corneas can all be transplanted to prolong or improve the quality of life. Joints can be replaced with artificial ones.

Perhaps the most remarkable advances have been in **key-hole surgery**. Compared to minor surgery, major operations increase the dangers of infection and shock, and take longer so more anaesthetic is needed. Using fibre optics, only small incisions need to be made, operations are often quicker and recovery time is reduced (see Source 10).

SOURCE 11
The largest causes of 'lost potential years of life', 1986 to 1990

('Years of life lost' assumes people will live to 75 years old. If they die when they are 50 they will have lost 25 'potential years of life'.)

Heart disease: 43,323 years
Cancer: 55,211 years
Strokes: 8,799 years
Motor vehicle accidents: 5,659 years
Smoking was reported to have contributed to one-sixth of all deaths.

From the Report of the Director of Public Health for Sheffield, *1992.*

Public health and living conditions

Better housing is vital to peoples' well being. Back-to-back houses and slum areas are still being cleared. Proper drains and disposal of waste, as well as cleaner drinking water, have improved hygiene. Houses are now warmer, drier and less overcrowded.

The Clean Air Act of 1956 has brought to an end the suffocating smogs which so badly polluted Britain's cities. (Although pollution still exists.)

Health and Safety at work has played a part in reducing the risks of serious injury.

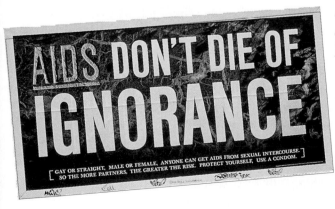

SOURCE 12 ▲
As the 20th century ends and the 21st century begins AIDS is a great threat to human health.

What threatens health at the end of the 20th century?

Some diseases, such as measles, smallpox, tuberculosis and diphtheria are now less of a threat. However, by 1970, heart disease and cancer were becoming major causes of death in Britain (see Source 11) because of:

• an ageing population (twice as many people are over 65 at the end of the century than at the beginning). Older people are more affected by heart problems and cancers;
• smoking and drug abuse;
• poor diets and lack of exercise;
• pollution, very often caused by vehicle exhausts.

A newly identified health threat is the complex virus **HIV** which can lead to **AIDS** (Acquired Immune Deficiency Syndrome). AIDS has spread throughout the world with alarming speed. As yet there is no cure for this disease which destroys the body's ability to fight infections (see Source 12). Drug companies are spending millions of pounds on research into finding a drug to combat it.

Rising costs of medical treatment and research can mean it is difficult for doctors to decide how money should be spent. Might this mean that the state cannot afford to look after people from 'the cradle to the grave'?

Living conditions could still be better. Poverty, poor housing and unemployment still undermine the nation's health.

Life expectancy has improved. A century ago it was 44 years for men, 48 years for women. Today, for a male born in the 1980s it is 72 years and, for a female, 78 years. Infant mortality fell dramatically as living standards improved and old diseases were conquered. Even so, medicine has further battles to fight.

Questions

1. What have been the most important factors in improving life expectancy in the late 20th century?

2. Is medicine just about more advanced technology to help doctors?

3. Despite the advances in medical science, what are the main threats to health at the end of the 20th century?

13 POVERTY

13.1 *How did local government deal with the problem of poverty before 1834*

SOURCE 1
This source describes Stafford workhouse (shown below). It comes from a visitor's letter to the Gentleman's Magazine.

THIS SECTION ANSWERS:

13.1 *How did local government deal with the problem of poverty before 1834?*

13.2 *How successful was the New Poor Law?*

13.3 *What were the effects of the New Poor Law?*

13.4 *How and why did attitudes towards the poor change?*

13.5 *How and why did the Liberal Governments help the poor from 1906-1914?*

13.6 *Why was there so much poverty in the 1920s and 30s?*

13.7 *Why were more Welfare Reforms introduced in the 1940s and how successful were they?*

Poverty exists when people, for whatever reason, are unable to provide themselves with the basic essentials of life – food, clothing and shelter. During the 18th and early 19th centuries, most workers – particularly farm workers in the south of England – experienced poverty at some time in their lives. People who were so poor they could not survive without help from their local parish were known as **paupers**.

What were the causes of poverty?

● The process of enclosure had led to a number of farm labourers being unemployed, or receiving insufficient wages to live on. Villagers also lost the use of the common land which they had used for grazing their animals, and collecting fuel for free.
● Shortages of corn in the 1790s, due to a reduction in grain imports as a result of the French Wars, and a series of bad harvests led to high bread prices. Bread formed the main part of people's diet, but while their wages remained low they could not afford these high bread prices. This particularly affected agricultural workers in the south of England.
● Some people could not work because of old age, sickness and disability. No work meant no income. Saving money was not common, so these people relied on others to help them in times of need.
● Unemployment, due to trade depressions, resulted in a severe drop in living standards.

How did the Old Poor Law work?

The treatment of the poor between 1601 and 1834 was based on the 1601 Elizabethan Poor Law Act.

- Each parish had to look after its own poor.
- To pay for this, householders paid a special tax – the **Poor Rate**.
- Overseers of the poor collected the Poor Rate, and distributed relief (help) to the poor.
- Two main kinds of relief were provided: **'indoor relief'** – when paupers were given relief in the workhouses and **'outdoor relief'** – when paupers were given relief in their own homes.

Initially this system had worked. However, over the years a number of changes were made. By the late 18th century treatment of the poor varied from area to area (see Sources 1 and 2). In 1782, Gilbert's Act allowed parishes to join together and form unions to build one large central workhouse. This was because only a few parishes could afford to build their own workhouse. However, few parishes took advantage of this Act, and by 1834 only 924 parishes had combined to make 67 **Gilbert Unions**.

In the 1790s there was growing concern about the hardship faced by agricultural labourers in the south of England. Allowance scales had been adopted as a way of helping labourers through this difficult time. The scale most commonly used was the **Speenhamland System**.

Stafford, Oct. 31, 1805

My Dear Friend

I wish I could pass the Borough Workhouse here over in silence but the state is really deplorable. The poor, 17 in number, cost 3 shillings and 3 pence per head for washing, soap and heating. The building is very old, almost tumbling down, the rooms and casements small, the ceilings low, the bedding old and dirty. There is no sick room. The women told me that about four years ago a fever broke out in it and out of 48 persons 22 died of it. The lower rooms are very damp, the upper dark and dirty.

With cordial esteem and regard,

believe me yours truly,

JAMES NEILD

KEY IDEAS

- Many agricultural labourers were poor
- The Old Poor Law was not working
- Treatment of the poor varied from area to area
- The Speenhamland System encouraged laziness and large families
- A Royal Commission of Inquiry was set up in 1832

SOURCE 2

A description of a Norfolk workhouse from The State of the Poor *written in 1797.*

The present number in the House is 539.

The men are employed in cultivating 60 acres of fields and gardens and weaving articles of wool, flax and hemp into various goods principally for use in the House.

The women and children are mostly employed in spinning.

No persons over 60 years of age are obliged to work.

The rooms are lofty, well aired and seem well adapted to the different purposes for which they are intended.

125

How did the Speenhamland System work?

Magistrates at Speen in Berkshire were anxious to prevent the suffering of agricultural labourers which might result in riots. In 1795 they decided that labourers' wages would be made up to subsistence level by the parish, according to the price of bread and the number of children in the family (see Source 3). This system quickly spread through parishes in south and south-east England. It was not used in the north where people were employed in factories, and wages were comparatively high.

The effects of the Speenhamland System

Good

● It saved many people from starvation.
● It kept workers quiet at a time of high prices and low wages.
● The problem of poverty was brought to the attention of rate payers.

Bad

● It encouraged labourers to be lazy as they could get just as much money by not working (see Source 4 and 5).
● Employers kept wages low as they knew workers' incomes would be made up by the parish.
● It encouraged people to have many children.
● Poor Rates went up alarmingly.

Why did the Poor Law need changing by 1834?

There were many reasons for this:
● In the early 19th century, the treatment of the poor was still based on the 1601 Elizabethan Poor Law. It was inadequate to cope with the rising population, and the migration of people from the countryside to the towns. In 1601, when the population was low, overseers had known the genuine cases of poverty. However, as the population increased, and towns expanded, it was impossible to know all the genuine cases.
● The allowance systems introduced in the 1790s did give relief to starving families, but they also encouraged labourers to be idle and have lots of children – as is shown in Source 5. The number of paupers increased as many able-bodied labourers claimed relief unnecessarily.

SOURCE 3

A labourer with a wife and three children earns 6s (30p) per week. The price of a gallon loaf of bread is 1s (5p). Under the allowance:

a man should have
$\qquad$ 3s $\qquad$ (15p)

his wife should have
$\qquad$ 1/6d $\qquad$ (7$\frac{1}{2}$p)

each child should have
$\qquad$ 1/6d $\qquad$ (7$\frac{1}{2}$p)
$\qquad$ 1/6d $\qquad$ (7$\frac{1}{2}$p)
$\qquad$ 1/6d $\qquad$ (7$\frac{1}{2}$p)

TOTAL $\qquad$ 9s $\qquad$ (45p)

This man really needs 9s (45p) a week for his family to live. As he only earns 6s (30p) the Parish makes up the labourer's wage by 3s (15p).

SOURCE 4

Thomas Pearce, a Sussex Labourer described how easy it was for fit men to gain relief:

Question:
'In your parish are there many able-bodied men upon the parish?'
Pearce: 'There are a great many men in our parish who like it better than being at work.'
Question:
'Why do they like it better?'
Pearce: 'They get the same money and don't do half so much work. They don't work like me; they be'ant at it so many hours, and they don't do so much work when they be at it; they're doing no good, and are only waiting for dinner-time and night; they be'ant working, it's only waiting.'

- The cost of Poor Relief was increasing rapidly. In 1818 the cost of caring for the poor had risen to nearly £8 million. This was four times the amount it had been in 1785. People who paid the Poor Rate criticised the Poor Laws because they did not like paying more tax.
- At the same time the labourers were demanding higher wages and increased poor relief allowances. During the Swing Riots in 1830 (see page 29) farmers and overseers were threatened, and property destroyed.

Steps leading to the 1834 Poor Law Report

The Government, alarmed at the rising cost of Poor Relief and shaken by the Swing Riots, realised that the Poor Law was not working. In 1832 it set up a Royal Commission of Inquiry to report on the Poor Laws and to recommend changes to the Poor Law system.

- In 1832 a Royal Commission of Inquiry was set up.
- 26 Assistant Commissioners were appointed to investigate the Poor Laws.
- 3,000 parishes were visited by the Commissioners.
- People in the parishes were questioned about the Poor Law.
- The findings were written up by Edwin Chadwick, the secretary to the Comission, and Nassau Senior.
- The Poor Law Report was published in 1834.

The Secretary of the Commission was Edwin Chadwick. He was an unpopular reformer who wanted to end the Speenhamland System. The Poor Law Report was strongly influenced by his views. The Report recommended that the Speenhamland System and outdoor relief should be abolished. Instead, poor relief should only be given in the workhouse. Conditions there were to be made so harsh that only those in desperate need would want to go in. Some historians think that the report was rushed and one-sided. However, the Government accepted most of its findings and, in August 1834, passed the **New Poor Law**.

SOURCE 5

An extract from The Saturday Magazine, *15 June 1833:*

Is not the Allowance System a great hardship to the careful and hard working man, making him no better off than the laziest fellow in his parish? Is it not a hardship that his thoughtless, careless, idle neighbour, because he chooses to marry and have a large family, is sure of being highly paid from his parish funds, whilst the man who is willing to work can find no one to employ him, even at the lowest rate, because the employers have to pay in rates much more than fair wages to the married neighbour and his family? By system of Allowance, the labourer is not rewarded according to his character. He is either reduced to unfairly low wages, or receives, as a charity from his parish, what should be paid him as the price of his work by his employer.

13.2 How successful was the New Poor Law?

The New Poor Law 1834

The aims of the New Poor Law were to:
- save money;
- reduce the number of paupers;
- restore self respect to working men;
- make the system uniform throughout the country.

- **At a national level.** A Poor Law Commission was based in London. This consisted of three members who would draw up instructions on how the workhouses were to be run.
- **At a local level:** Parishes were grouped together to form 'unions'. Each union was to have a Board of Guardians elected by rate payers who would run the workhouses. The Board of Guardians were often rate payers so they had an interest in keeping costs low.
- **All allowance systems**, including the Speenhamland System were ended.
- Only **indoor relief** was available for the able bodied poor (those fit for work). Life in the workhouse was deliberately made unpleasant and harsh so that it would discourage all but the most destitute. This was known as the 'Principle of Less Eligibility' which meant that conditions in the workhouse were to be less comfortable than in the homes of even the lowest-paid labourers. This view is shown in Source 6.
- **Outdoor relief** was stopped.

Effects of the New Poor Law

- Costs went down.
- The number of paupers decreased.
- Men worked harder in order to avoid for themselves, and their families, the shame and hardship of the workhouse.
- There was not as much variation from area to area as to how the poor were treated. From the Government's point of view the law

SOURCE 6

An extract from an article written in the early 1830s entitled The Present State of the Poor Law.

The poorhouse ought to be run in such a way that the labouring population see it as less comfortable than their homes. I wish to see the poorhouse looked to with dread by our labouring classes. Let the poor see and feel that their parish, although it will not let them die through absolute want, is yet the hardest taskmaster and the most harsh and unkind friend they can apply to.

was very successful. However, the law ignored the unavoidable cases of poverty. If people were poor, it was thought to be their fault and due to some weakness of character. That was not true. There were many people who were poor, through no fault of their own, for reasons such as sickness or old age. Much poverty was also only temporary, especially in the north of England where – although workers earned higher wages in the factories – they were affected by trade cycles. This resulted in brief periods of unemployment.

There was so much opposition to the New Poor Law that it became the most hated law of the 19th century. The workhouses were known as 'Bastilles' (the French prison where conditions were very harsh).

The Rev. Joseph Raynor Stephens said in a speech at Newcastle-under-Lyme, in 1838 about the Poor Law Amendment Act:

The people were not going to stand this. Rather than wife and husband, father and son, should be separated and jailed, and fed on skillee [thin porridge], sooner than wife or daughter should wear the prison dress, Newcastle ought to be one blaze of fire, with only one way to put it out, and that with the blood of all who supported this abominable law.

Why did people hate the workhouses?

Conditions inside the workhouse were harsher than the worst conditions outside. Different kinds of people were mixed together in the workhouse – sick, healthy, young, old, tramps, prostitutes, mentally ill people and criminals. People in workhouses lived under strict rules:

● Families were split up (this was one of the worst things).

● Uniforms had to be worn like in prisons (poor people disliked this as they felt that because they were poor they were being treated as criminals).

● Food was limited and meals had to be eaten in silence.

● Smoking and drinking were not allowed.

● Boring tasks had to be performed such as oakum picking (untwisting old ropes to tease out the fibre, called oakum, so that it could be reused in the seams of boats to make them watertight – Source 8), stone breaking and bone crushing.

Disraeli, Prime Minister in the late 19th century said, *'the 1834 Act announced to the world that in England poverty was a crime'.* Being a pauper was a bigger disgrace than ever before – people would rather starve than enter the workhouse.

How did people oppose the law?

● In 1837 trade was bad and many workers were laid off through no fault of their own. However, they were only entitled to relief if they went into the workhouses. Workers in northern towns refused to go, and Boards of Guardians in many areas were forced to give relief to the able bodied outside the workhouse.

● Anti-Poor Law Committees were set up to organise resistance to the law. They were led by strong-minded individuals such as the Reverend Joseph Raynor Stephens (Source 7) and Richard Oastler.

● *The Times* published articles criticising the law.

● The harshness of the New Poor Law was attacked by Charles Dickens in his 1838 novel *Oliver Twist* (see Source 12 page 131).

● Many workers joined the Chartist Movement in the belief that, if they could get working-class representation in Parliament, then the law would be abolished (see pages 148-149).

The New Poor Law remained the basis of Poor Relief until the early 20th century. Yet although conditions in the workhouses were very harsh, not all were cruel. However, one of the greatest fears of the poor after 1834 was that they might end their days in a workhouse.

SOURCE 8 ▲

Oakum picking. (This picture shows prisoners at work. which highlights the similarity between life in the workhouse and prison.)

		BREAKFAST		DINNER						SUPPER	
		Bread	Porridge	Bread	Cooked meat	veg.	Scouse Broth	Porridge	(stew)	Bread	Broth
		ozs	pints	ozs	ozs	ozs	pints	pints	pints	ozs	pints
Sun.	Men	4	2	4	5	12	1½	–	–	4	2
	Women	4	1½	4	4	10	1½	–	–	4	1½
Mon.	Men	4	2	4	–	–	–	2	–	4	2
	Women	4	1½	4	–	–	–	1½	–	4	1½
Tues.	Men	4	2	4	–	–	–	–	2	4	2
	Women	4	1½	4	–	–	–	–	1½	4	1½
Wed.	Men	4	2	4	–	–	–	2	–	4	2
	Women	4	1½	4	–	–	–	1½	–	4	1½
Thur.	Men	4	2	4	5	12	1½	–	–	4	2
	Women	4	1½	4	4	10	1½	–	–	4	1½
Fri.	Men	4	2	4	–	–	–	2	–	4	2
	Women	4	1½	4	–	–	–	1½	–	4	1½
Sat.	Men	4	2	4	–	–	–	–	2	4	2
	Women	4	1½	4	–	–	–	–	1½	4	1½

SOURCE 9 ▲
The workhouse diet from the Lancashire town of Clitheroe, 1852.

Questions

1. What do Sources 4 and 5 (pages 126-127) tell us about the defects of The Speenhamland System?

2. The following are all reasons why The Poor Law Royal Commission of Inquiry was set up in 1832:

   - the increasing number of poor people
   - the rising cost of poor relief
   - the encouragement of larger families
   - the effects of the Swing Riots.

   Are they equally important in bringing about the Poor Law Amendment Act of 1834?

3. What were the main aims of the Government in passing the New Poor Law?

4. Read Source 6. Give two ways in which The New Poor Law set out to make the workhouses 'looked to with dread' by the labouring classes.

5. Why did many people only enter the workhouse as a last resort?

6. Read Source 9. Was it possible to remain healthy on such a diet?

7. In what ways was the New Poor Law different from the Old Poor Law?

SOURCE ENQUIRY

13.3 *What were the effects of the New Poor Law* ?

◄ **SOURCE 10**
Refuge for the Poor – Male Ward, 1843.

The New Poor Law resulted in many different comments on its effects.

THE WORKHOUSE

SOURCE 11

Extracts from Baxter's Book of the Bastilles, *which was a collection of information chosen to show the New Poor Law in a bad light:*

A little boy having been separated from his mother in Nottingham Union raged in despair and tore off his hair by the handful.

At Bourne, a poor man applied to the Guardians for relief. They offered him a place in the workhouse, but he refused. A week later he was found dead in a field, having chosen death by starvation rather than enter a workhouse under the present system.

SOURCE 12
▼ *An illustration from* Oliver Twist, *by Charles Dickens, 1838.*

131

SOURCE ENQUIRY

SOURCE 13 ▼

*A Poor Law Inspector
reported in 1839:*

Recently there was a rumour going about that the children in the workhouses were killed to make pies with, while the old, when dead, were used to manure the fields in order to spare the expense of coffins.

HORROR STORIES

SOURCE 14 ▼

In 1845 an inmate of the Andover Workhouse made this statement:

To satisfy our hunger a little, we ate the rotting and stinking meat off the bones that had been brought in. I have seen a man eat raw horse flesh off the bones.

SOURCE 15 ▼

The Guardians of the Cheadle Poor Law Union wrote in 1838:

We are likewise confident that there will be a considerable fall in the Poor Rates. We would not rejoice in this decrease if the poor were harmed but we are certain that no such result will take place.

SOURCE 16 ▼

The Guardians of St. Ives Union wrote to the Home Secretary in March 1837 expressing satisfaction at the working of the New Act:

From practical experience we can state that:

(1) the condition of the aged and infirm poor has been improved;

(2) a beneficial change is gradually developing itself amongst all classes of paupers;

(3) a very great saving of expense has come to the ratepayers;

(4) few able-bodied men in the Union are now out of employ although prior to the formation of the Union a great number of able-bodied men were receiving parish relief. We felt that the poor of this Union in general are much improved in their morals and habits.

SOURCE 17 ▼

The Rev. Henry Kelson of the Folkington Union wrote in Operation of the Poor Law Amendment Act in the County of Sussex, *1836:*

FINANCIAL SAVINGS

The annual average expenditure in the parishes forming this Union, for the years ending 1831–32 and 33 … produces £16,643 … an average monthly expenditure of £1,386, while a similar average on the Union expenditure, including the repairs and alteration to the workhouses, will be found not to exceed £550 being a difference of £836 per month, by which it will be seen a saving of £10,000 per annum will be effected …

SOURCE 18 ▼

A visitor to a Manchester workhouse in the 1860s made these notes:

There is not an able-bodied inmate of this workhouse at the moment. it is almost empty and will not be filled till the winter. They prefer their home and their freedom at any price. They cannot bear being shut up and subjected to discipline. They prefer to be free and starve. The workhouse is regarded as a prison and the poor consider it a point of honour not to go there.

HUMAN SUFFERING

SOURCE 19 ▼

This extract from a poem written in 1846 by James Withen Reynolds, a pauper in the workhouse, shows his feeling of despair:

I sometimes look up to the bit of blue sky
High over my head with a tear in my eye
Surrounded by walls that are too high to climb
Confined like a felon without any crime

SOURCE 20 ▼

In his autobiography, When I was a child, an old potter described how, when his father was unable to find work during a strike in 1840, the family had to go into Chell workhouse in Burslem:

Early in the morning we left home by the field road to Chell, to avoid being seen. None of us wanted to go, but we must go to our new home. The very vastness of it chilled us. Our reception was more chilling still. The younger ones huddled more closely to their parents, from fear of those stern officials. Doors were unlocked and the sound of locks and keys and bars and doors banging froze the blood within us. We finally landed in a cellar, clean and bare, and as grim as a prison cell. We youngsters were roughly disrobed, and roughly washed, and roughly attired in rough clothes. Then we parted, the young ones being taken one way and the parents (separated too) taken as well to different regions in that merciful establishment. We might have committed some unnameable crime, or carried some dreadful infection.

Questions

1. What can you learn about conditions in the workhouse from Source 10?

2. Read Source 11. Give two aspects of the New Poor Law which this source illustrates.

3. Give four ways in which the writer of Source 16 believes that the New Poor Law was successful.

4. Sources 15 and 18 say different things about the effects of the New Poor Law. Does this mean that one of them must be inaccurate? Explain your answer.

5. Read Sources 15 and 16. To what extent do these sources give similar impressions about the effects of the New Poor Law?

6. How useful is Source 20 to a historian studying the workings of the New Poor Law?

7. What problems would a modern historian have in using Sources 14 and 19 when writing about conditions in the workhouse?

8. 'The New Poor Law was a success because the amount spent on Poor Relief dropped dramatically.' Using the sources and what you have learnt on the New Poor Law explain whether or not you agree with this statement.

13.4 How and why did attitudes towards the poor change ?

In Victorian times many people thought that poverty was the fault of the individual and that, if someone was poor, it was the result of laziness, or of wasting money on gambling and drink. *Self Help,* written by Samuel Smiles in 1859, had confirmed this viewpoint by saying that people ought to be able to live independently without having to rely on the support of anyone else.

Towards the end of the 19th century this attitude towards poverty began to change. Many books and articles were written about the living and working conditions of the poor. The view was now that, for most people, poverty was not their fault. Instead it was the result of forces they could not control such as sickness, old age, low wages and unemployment.

Many people contributed towards the change in attitude towards the poor. This change led to several charities being set up.

Henry Mayhew (1812-1887) published *London Labour* and *The London Poor* in 1861 which highlighted the poverty and squalor of London. The Government took no notice as they still believed poverty was caused by laziness.

Dr John Barnardo (1845-1905) was a preacher from Dublin. He was shocked at the large number of children roaming the London streets.

He rented a house in Stepney, London for twelve boys in 1866, and set up the first **Barnardo's Children's Home** in 1870. The aim was to care for, discipline and educate children. No child was ever turned away. By 1900 Barnardo had opened over a hundred homes to provide shelter for homeless and orphaned children.

KEY IDEAS

- Victorians blamed poverty on weakness of character
- Dr Barnardo set up his Children's Homes
- William Booth founded the Salvation Army
- In 1889 a third of London's population was living in poverty
- Evidence linked sickness and low wages to poverty

SOURCE 21
Booth preaching. ▲

SOURCE 22 ▲
'Before' and 'after' photographs of a Barnado's boy.

William Booth (1829-1912) was a Methodist Minister in London's East End trying to convert people to Christianity. He was shocked at the conditions of the slums and he founded the **Salvation Army** in 1876. He saw running this organisation as a war on sin and poverty. He realised that poorly-dressed working class men felt uncomfortable mixing with a well-dressed congregation in church, so his main aim was to take the 'gospel of love' to the slums.

Booth used to say, 'I like my tea as I like my religion – hot!' and recruited a group of 'soldiers' who set out to make religion cheerful. They sang joyful hymns accompanied by lively music (see Source 23). In 1890 he published a book *Darkest England* in which he said more was known about Africa than the slums of Britain. He urged people to look at life in the industrial towns where slum dwellers were forced to live like savages.

Booth raised £100,000 from the sales of this book and used it to set up shelters and soup kitchens to provide help for the sick, homeless and unemployed. By the time Booth died in 1912, the Salvation Army had become a world-wide movement.

SOURCE 23 ▲
The Salvation Army spreading the 'gospel of love'.

135

Charles Booth (1840-1916) conducted the first detailed survey to prove that many people were living in poverty. Booth had worked out that a family, consisting of a man, wife and three children, would need an income of 21s 8d (£1.08) per week to be above the poverty line. His investigators visited London families asking them questions. All the evidence was written up, and, in 1889, he published the first of several reports. He found that a third of London's population lived in appalling poverty. He also reported that the main causes of poverty were old age, sickness, unemployment and low wages, not laziness and drink. Many people felt that London, being England's capital and its largest city, was exceptional. They refused to believe that the figures in Booth's report could be similar in other areas of the country.

Seebohm Rowntree (1871-1954) was the son of a cocoa and chocolate manufacturer in York. He was interested in the findings of Booth's report and decided to conduct a similar survey in York. The results of his work were published as *Poverty: A Study of Town Life*, in 1901 (Source 24). Rowntree found that 28% of the total population of York had incomes insufficient for the bare necessities. They did not have enough money to pay for food, rent, fuel and clothing – even if they spent every penny wisely. They certainly did not have any left over for items such as postage stamps, newspapers, tram rides or

tobacco. He also reported that (apart from people having large families) there were two main causes of poverty (see Source 26):
- The family's chief wage earner was ill, old or dead.
- Wages were too low.

In spite of Rowntree's report, many people still thought that gambling and drink were the causes of poverty. Rowntree disliked these vices but he suggested that men often took to gambling and drink, not because of a weakness of character, but to escape the terrible conditions in which they lived.

As a result of the work of Booth and Rowntree, there was definite evidence that poverty was widespread in Britain. The problem was too big to be solved by self-help and charity. The Government had to take action if the situation was to improve.

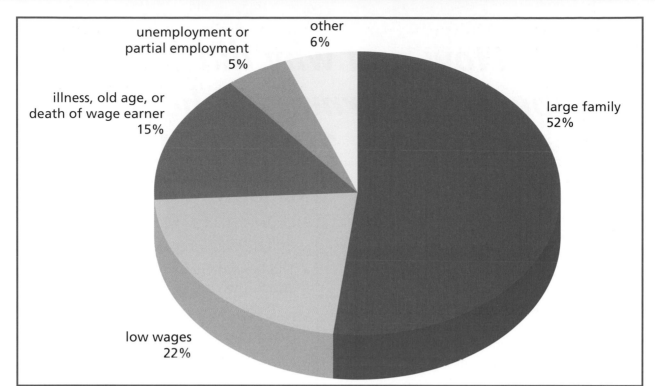

unemployment or
partial employment
5%

other
6%

illness, old age, or
death of wage earner
15%

large family
52%

low wages
22%

◀ **SOURCE 25**
*The kitchen in a
poverty-stricken house.*

SOURCE 26 ▲
*Rowntree identified
these causes of
poverty.*

Questions

1. What do you understand by 'self help'?

2. Copy and complete the following table:

Person	Date	Work	Why important?
Henry Mayhew			
Dr Barnardo			
William Booth			
Charles Booth			
Joseph Rowntree			

3. Which person from the table made the most important contribution to changing people's attitude to poverty? Explain your answer.

4. In what ways was the work of Dr Barnardo and William Booth
    (a) similar?
    (b) different?

13.5 How and why did the Liberal Governments help the poor from 1906-1914?

In the 1906 general election, a Liberal Government was elected. It included David Lloyd George and Winston Churchill. The Government decided to pass laws to protect people from the causes and effects of poverty. This was a major change in attitude towards the poor. The laws that they passed to help children, the sick, unemployed and the elderly are known as the Liberal Reforms. These Reforms laid the foundations of the Welfare State.

A **Welfare State** exists when the Government sees it as its duty to care for those in need. Sickness benefits and pensions are regarded as a right.

SOURCE 27
The Liberal Reforms. ▼

KEY IDEAS

- Evidence had proved that poverty was widespread
- The Liberal Government wanted to attack the causes of poverty
- New laws helped children, the elderly, sick and unemployed
- Money was raised through taxation
- The foundations of the Welfare State were laid

Why did the Government introduce the Reforms?

The Government was influenced by changing ideas.
- **Socialism** was a growing movement. Socialists argued that the country's wealth should be more equally spread.
- Successful **strikes** from unskilled trade unions prompted reform (see pages 150-152).
- By 1900 most working class men had the vote. They would vote for whichever party was going to improve their living conditions.
- In 1906 the **Labour Party** was founded to represent the working classes in Parliament.

CHILDREN
1906 School Meals Act (daily cooked meal).
1907 School Medical Service.
1908 Children's Charter (including terms such as: children not to beg, under 16s not to go into pubs or be sold cigarettes, children sent to borstal not prison) .

THE SICK
1911 National Insurance Act – Part 1 (workers earning less than £160 per year were insured against sickness. They had to pay 4d out of their weekly wage. Each payment earned them a 'stamp' on their card. The employer contributed 3d worth of stamps and the Government a further 2d).

UNEMPLOYED
1909 Labour Exchanges (gave details of job vacancies).
1911 National Insurance Act – Part 2 (unemployment benefit for workers in ship-building, iron founding and construction industries. Again the workers, employers and the Government each paid contributions).

THE ELDERLY
1908 Old Age Pensions Act (a state pension of 25p per week was given to people over 70 whose income was less than £21 per year).

SOURCE 28

Winston Churchill said in 1906:

Our cause is the cause of the left out millions. We are all agreed that the State must concern itself with the care of the sick, of the aged and above all of the children.

• In 1902 half of the new recruits for the Boer War were found to be suffering from malnutrition.

• The evidence collected from the surveys of Booth and Rowntree had proved that poverty was widespread.

A Poor Law Commission ran from 1905-1909, looking into the workings of the Poor Law. Two reports were issued, because the members could not agree over the causes of poverty. The 'Majority Report' said that gambling and drink were the main causes of poverty. The 'Minority Report' said that poverty was due to circumstances beyond the control of the individual. The Government took no direct action on the recommendations of the Commission, but they did pass some very important reforms (see Source 27).

How were the Reforms paid for?

The Government obtained the money by taxation. In 1909 the People's Budget raised new taxes, and placed duties on spirits, tobacco and motoring. There was opposition to the Budget from the rich, but the House of Lords finally accepted it.

Importance of the Reforms

• This was the first time taxation was used to help the poor.

• The Government had accepted that the State should protect its citizens from the hardships caused by sickness, unemployment and old age.

• The Old Age Pensions were the first nation-wide service. As Lloyd George said, 'We are lifting the shadow of the workhouse from the homes of the poor'.

Questions

1. What do you understand by the term 'Welfare State'?

2. Read Source 28.
   (a) Who is Churchill referring to when he says 'Our Cause'?
   (b) How has the attitude towards the poor changed from that of the early 19th century?
   (c) Which part of society did Churchill consider needed most care?

3. Copy and complete the following table by writing an Act in the space:

ACT	EFFECT
	Improved the health of children
	Would help to stop the elderly going into the workhouse
	Improved the diet of children
	Would stop workers going from factory to factory looking for work

4. 'The following were all equally important in helping the poor between 1906 and 1914:
   (a) The Old Age Pensions Act, 1908;
   (b) Setting up Labour Exchanges, 1909;
   (c) The National Insurance Act, 1911.'
   Do you agree? Explain your answer with reference to (a) (b), and (c).

SOURCE 29

This extract from a speech made by David Lloyd George in 1912, refers to an Act of Parliament passed in 1911:

So long as the head of the family is in good health, on the whole, with a fierce struggle, he can keep hunger from the door; but when he breaks down in health there is no one to fight for the young. What happens in these cases? In hundreds of thousands there is absolute poverty, everything going from the household, nothing left unpawned, except its pride.

On Monday next an Act of Parliament comes into operation that abolishes that state of things forever.

13.6 Why was there so much poverty in the 1920s and 30s?

The main cause of poverty during the inter-war years was unemployment (see Source 29). Unemployment started to rise in 1920. Men were laid off because of a drop in trade, especially in the traditional industries of coal, iron, steel, textiles and ship-building. Britain had suffered from competition with America, Germany and France since the late 19th century. While Britain's industries were involved in the First World War, some overseas customers were lost to competitors. Between 1920 and 1922 the unemployment figures rose sharply.

Unemployment reached its peak during the **Great Depression** in 1929-33. After the Wall Street Crash in New York, the American Government stopped lending money to Europe, and increased customs duties on imports. This plunged the world into deep recession. British factories closed down, and unemployment rose again rapidly. By 1932 there were nearly 3 million unemployed.

This did not affect the whole country evenly. The north-east of England, Lancashire, South Wales and the Lowlands of Scotland were hardest hit because they were the centres of the declining industries – coal, iron and steel, shipbuilding and textiles. In 1927 there was 31% unemployment in South Wales. The effect of the Depression was less significant in the Midlands and south of England because these areas had new industries such as cars, chemicals, electrical goods and aviation.

October 1929	1,200,000
March 1930	1,600,000
July 1930	2,100,000
August 1931	3,100,000

KEY IDEAS

- Unemployment was high between the wars
- Trade fell in the traditional industries
- Unemployment was highest in the north of England and South Wales
- Government action had little effect on poverty

How successful was the Government in dealing with poverty in the 1930s?

The second Labour Government, with Ramsay MacDonald as Prime Minister, was elected in 1929. By 1931 the Government was in trouble because unemployment benefit cost more than the money available. The Government took action to deal with the effects of the Great Depression.

- August 1931 – a National Government was set up with the aim of keeping spending down to a minimum.
- September 1931 – the budget reduced Government spending. Unemployment benefit was reduced by 10% and income tax was increased. The Government introduced the '**dole**' – extended unemployment benefit. To receive this, a '**means test**' had to be passed when an unemployed person's family income and savings were investigated.
- 1934 – national insurance was separated from assistance. Unemployment benefit returned to its 1931 level. Depressed areas, including South Wales and Tyneside, were made '**Special Areas**'. Firms starting factories in these areas were given tax and rate rebates, as well as financial grants. **Unemployment**

◀ SOURCE 30
Unemployment figures.

140

SOURCE 31

This comes from a book about the East End of London in the late 1920s and early 1930s:

The dole money wasn't enough to keep a cat alive. People would go to a market and bring home discarded vegetables and cut out the decaying parts so they could use the rest in stews. They would take good care that the neighbours never saw them doing this. The poor were ashamed of their poverty, God knows why, the shame wasn't theirs.

SOURCE 32 *Jarrow Crusade.* ▼

Assistance Boards took over running labour exchanges, the dole and the means test. Training schemes were set up and people were helped to find work in another area.

How did the poor react?

It was a very hard time for the unemployed and their families. At least the dole did stop families from starving. Some of the unemployed joined hunger strike marches, of which the most famous was '**The Jarrow Crusade**' in 1936. Two hundred unemployed ship workers marched from Jarrow in the north east to take a petition to London see Source 32). Three-quarters of the town's working population had been left unemployed when its shipyard closed. The marchers wanted the Government to do something, but it ignored their plea to open up new industries.

Attempts to remove poverty had little success. The means test was resented and regarded as humiliating. The Special Areas Act had limited success because the Government did not put enough money into the scheme. By 1934 the southern areas were recovering, but full employment did not return until the outbreak of the Second World War.

Questions

1. Study Source 30 and the text.
   (a) When was unemployment at its highest?
   (b) In which areas would most of these unemployed people live?
   (c) The unemployment figures had dropped by 1940? Why?

2. Read Source 31.
   (a) Give two ways in which unemployment affected people at this time.
   (b) To receive the dole the unemployed had to undergo a 'means test'. Why did they dislike the means test?

3. Study Source 32. How useful is this source for the study of poverty? Why did people join the Jarrow Crusade?

4. How did the Government react to the problems caused by unemployment?

Why were more Welfare Reforms introduced in the 1940s and how successful were they ?

The terrible poverty and unemployment that followed the First World War, persuaded many reformers, especially in the Labour Party, that more had to be done. The existing social services were muddled. There were different rates of benefit for the sick and unemployed.

In 1939, when the Second World War broke out, many young children were evacuated from cities to live in rural areas. Many middle class people, who had lived in villages most of their lives, were shocked to see dirty, deprived and badly-clothed city children. A feeling gradually developed that Britain would have to be made a better place to live when the war was over.

In June 1941, the wartime National Government asked Sir William Beveridge to draw up an insurance scheme to cover the whole population. The **Beveridge Report** was issued in December 1942.

Main features of the Report

● The Government should provide a 'Welfare State' by taking charge of all security from the 'cradle to the grave'.
● The plan would conquer the 'Five giants': want, disease, ignorance, squalor and idleness.
● All the previous insurance schemes would be replaced by one complete scheme covering all citizens whatever their income.
● Everyone working would pay a single weekly contribution recorded by a stamp. In return, benefits would be paid in cases of sickness, unemployment and old age – without any means test.

The Report was a best seller. Beveridge became a national hero

KEY IDEAS

● Existing social services were muddled

● People were shocked at the poverty of the evacuees

● Beveridge's Plan covered the whole population

● The Health Service nearly collapsed through a shortage of funds

● There is still great debate over the Welfare State

overnight. An American commented, '*Sir William, possibly next to Mr Churchill, is the most popular figure in Britain today*'. In July 1945 the Labour Party won the General Election, with a large majority, because they had promised to introduce the Welfare State.

SOURCE 33
Acts of Parliament which tackled the 'Five Giants'. ▼

WANT
1945 Family Allowances Act (25p per child per week – not the first child.)
1946 National Insurance Act (For a small weekly contribution gave out benefits when sick unemployed or retired – men aged 65, women aged 60. Additional benefits included funeral grants and maternity benefits. Benefits applied only to those working.)
1948 National Assistance Act (Those not working were covered by this National Assistance Act.)
DISEASE
1946 National Health Service (Free medical treatment and medicines for all.)

How successful were the Welfare Reforms?

● All branches of the health service were heavily used, because everyone could now receive free health care. This was a drain on funds. Charges for prescriptions, dental and ophthalmic services have since been introduced. Private medicine has expanded rapidly since the 1960s because of long National Health Service waiting lists for routine operations.

● In 1959 the Prime Minister Harold Macmillan claimed that people had 'never had it so good'. Yet poverty still existed, with the south generally prospering, and the north suffering from poverty and unemployment. Even by the 1960s, 3 million people were still living in unfit housing. In 1960 it was estimated that 14% of the population were living below the poverty line.

● Pressure has been put on the system by a population increased by the post-war baby boom and generally longer life-spans.

● Soaring inflation in the 1970s and increasing unemployment have again raised the issue of how the Welfare State is to be funded.

O, rare and refreshing Beveridge!

SOURCE 34
A Daily Mirror cartoon. ▲

The Welfare State is still the centre of a great debate. There are people who complain that not enough money is spent on welfare. However, there are also people who say that the Welfare State is no longer needed, that it is wrong to allow the well-off to draw benefits that they do not need, and that the Welfare State makes people lazy.

SOURCE 35

Winston Churchill, a Conservative MP and Prime Minister in the wartime Coalition Government, speaking after the publication of the Beveridge Report, *said:*

A dangerous optimism is growing up about conditions it will be possible to establish here after the war. Unemployment and low wages are to be abolished; great developments in housing and health will be undertaken. At the same time the cost of living is not to be raised. The Beveridge plan is to abolish want. The question steals across the mind whether we are not committing our 45 million people to tasks beyond them. While not disheartening our people, Ministers should, in my view, be careful not to raise false hopes.

IGNORANCE

1944 Education Act (Every child had a right to the best education.)

SQUALOR

1947 Town & Country Planning Act (Local councils had to provide more low rent housing. This resulted in prefabs and more council estates.)

1946 New Towns Act (Allowed new towns to be planned and built by development corporations.)

IDLENESS

A Policy was implemented towards full employment.

Questions

1. Why was the Beveridge Report needed?

2. Study Source 34. What can you learn about people's opinion of the Beveridge Report?

3. Study Source 35. Why was Winston Churchill not convinced about the proposals put forward in the Beveridge Report?

4. Study Sources 34 and 35. Does the fact that the opinions of the Beveridge Report in Sources 34 and 35 differ mean they are no use to a historian studying the Welfare Reforms? Explain your answer using the sources and the text.

14 TRADE UNIONS & WORKING CLASS MOVEMENTS

14.1 What attempts were made to organise the working classes in the early 19th century?

An early name for a trade union was a '**combination**', and there could be combinations (groups) of employers as well as workers. Workers' combinations would try to get better working conditions and pay, generally by threatening strikes by their members.

For years, skilled craftsmen such as printers, carpenters and silkweavers had formed local associations or trade clubs to protect their members' interests. **Trade clubs** were the forerunners of trade unions, and many also provided friendly society benefits. **Friendly Societies** were mainly small, local organisations, offering a kind of self help before there was a Welfare State. It was the better-paid, more skilled workers who formed friendly societies. In return for weekly subscriptions they received cash benefits in times of need.

Early trade unions had to struggle against Government regulation and employers' hostility. In 1799-1800 the Government passed the **Combination Acts** which made combinations of workers or employers illegal (Source 2).

SOURCE 1
A cartoonist's impression of 'Peterloo'. (Look at the picture of the Battle of Waterloo on page 15.) ▲

Why did the Government pass the Combination Acts?

The Government was worried about:

• **the growing strength of the trade clubs and societies.** By the end of the 18th century some groups of workers, like hatters and sailmakers, were sending petitions to Parliament demanding fair pay and better conditions.

• **food shortages** due to bad harvests, interruptions of trade and high prices. The shortages had resulted in more working class combinations demanding higher wages.

• **the French Revolution in 1789.** The Government feared that the working class would also rise in revolution in Britain.

'Peterloo'

Many societies carried on as before, or continued in secret. The Combination Acts did not destroy working class protest. The French Wars ended with Napoleon's defeat at Waterloo in 1815. Between 1815 and 1819 depression hit many industries, resulting in low wages and unemployment. The poor harvests of 1817 and 1818 made matters worse. People began to demand political change because ordinary workers had no vote and no say in how the country was run.

In August 1819, 60,000 people gathered at St Peter's Fields, Manchester to listen to Henry Hunt, the powerful speaker for political reform. The magistrates panicked at the size of the crowd, and ordered the Manchester Yeomanry to arrest Hunt. In the confusion which followed, eleven people were killed and over four hundred wounded (see Source 1). The tragedy was called 'Peterloo' because soldiers had attacked the meeting as if it had been the French army at Waterloo, and the Government seemed just as pleased about the event. There was severe criticism of the Government but it was still afraid of radical workers. In December 1819 it passed the '**Six Acts**' which, among other things, gave magistrates the power to ban outside meetings and marches.

Why were the Combination Acts repealed in 1824?

Francis Place, a London tailor, led the movement for repeal. Through the support of MP Joseph Hume, a Parliamentary Select Committee was set up in 1824 to look at the question of repeal. The fear of revolution was now over. Combinations and peaceful bargaining seemed acceptable. The Committee recommended repeal which took place in 1824. Trade unions were now legal.

SOURCE 2

Part of the Combination Acts said:

All contracts and agreements between workmen for obtaining an increase in wages, or reducing their hours of work or for preventing a master from employing whomsoever he likes are declared illegal.

Why was the Grand National Consolidated Trades Union (GNCTU) formed?

As industry developed, unions became increasingly relevant to working people. Because large numbers of people worked together in factories, it was easier to form unions.

Robert Owen, the mill owner and social reformer, decided that if small unions joined together to form one large union for all workers (the GNCTU) they could put more pressure on the Government to change things. The aims of the GNCTU were to:

● stop pay cuts;
● shorten hours;
● stop work for a month so that industry would be ruined, the capitalist system destroyed, and the government would collapse;
● give the working classes more say in production.

At first the idea appealed to the workers and by June 1834 there were over half a million members.

What action was taken by employers and the Government?

● The idea of one large union worried employers and the Government.
● Many employers made workers sign a declaration (called the 'document') saying that they did not, or would not, belong to a union (see Source 3).

● Some employers used **lock-outs**. They refused to let the employees into work until they agreed to certain employment conditions.
● In March 1834 some farm labourers from Tolpuddle in Dorset formed a branch of the Agricultural Labourers Union. New members were enrolled in secret ceremonies. The labourers wanted to increase their very low wages. Their leader George Loveless explained at his trial, '*We were uniting together to preserve ourselves, our wives and our children from utter degradation and starvation*'. The Government, worried about the GNCTU, decided to make an example of this union to discourage others from joining. Loveless and five others were accused of swearing secret oaths and sentenced to seven years transportation to Australia. They were known as the '**Tolpuddle Martyrs**'.

Why did the GNCTU fail?

● Action by employers and the punishment of the Tolpuddle Martyrs put workers off joining trade unions.
● Owen was not a successful leader. The union was badly organised and its aims were not clear to members.
● Many refused to pay the 1s (5p) a week membership so there was not enough money to sustain a long strike.

SOURCE 4 ▲
*An illustration showing a
protest meeting against
the transportation of the
Tolpuddle Martyrs, 1834.*

SOURCE 5

The meat was bad. The butchers
put fresh blood on old joints and
powdered the fat white. The worst
meat was kept in the back yard until
it was dark and sold by candle light.

From a parliamentary report, 1842.

- Poor communications made a
national organisation impossible at
this time.
- Different trades were not interested
in the demands of others.
- The workers were more interested
in immediate gains, such as more pay,
than Owen's long-term ideas.
- Four of the biggest unions did not
support the GNCTU.

By 1835 the GNCTU had collapsed.
The early trade union movement had,
therefore, failed. It had made little
progress since 1800 except to
become legal.

Why did the early trade union movement fail?

- It was restricted by laws.
- Government and employers
were hostile.
- The working classes had no internal unity.
- Most factory workers were ill-educated.
- Most workers were afraid of losing their jobs.

From 1834 to 1850 unions grew only slowly. Working men
joined other movements, including the Co-operative Movement
and the Chartists.

What was the Co-operative Movement?

The Co-op shops of today date back to the 1840s. In 1844
the '**Rochdale Pioneers**' opened a shop in Rochdale to sell
groceries. In the early 19th century food was often expensive
and of very poor quality, as Source 5 shows. The aim of the
Rochdale Pioneers was to sell good food at reasonable prices.
At first there were 28 members paying 2d a week. Anyone
could join as long as they paid a small deposit. After the
trading profit was known, members got a dividend (a share
of the profits) according to how much they spent in the shop.
The idea was copied by others. By 1851 there were 130 retail
societies with a total of 15,000 members.

14.2 Did Chartism fail?

The Chartist Movement

This was mainly a working-class movement, which aimed at improving living and working conditions through the control of Parliament. It started in 1836 with the formation of the London Working Men's Association. The secretary was William Lovett. At a meeting in Birmingham in 1838, Lovett, Feargus O'Connor, Thomas Attwood and Francis Place helped to draw up a list of rights and a programme of reform. They issued a 'charter' of six aims:

- vote for all men over 21;
- secret ballots;
- no property qualification for MPs;
- payment of MPs;
- constituencies to be of equal size;
- annual parliamentary elections.

Why did so many join the movement?

A Reform Act was passed in 1832, leaving many working-class supporters of reform disappointed, because they did not receive the vote. Two years later, following the 1834 Poor Law Act, attempts to establish Poor Law Unions, and harsh workhouse conditions were bitterly resented. Trade unions did not provide an answer to these problems.

The movement was particularly supported by workers in the industrial Midlands and the North. They wanted improved living conditions in towns, and improved working conditions in factories. They were also concerned about high food prices, especially for bread.

Methods used by the Chartists

Differences began to appear in the methods chosen to achieve their aims. Lovett and Attwood favoured winning public and parliamentary support by processions, demonstrations and petitions. Others, including O'Connor, wanted a general strike leading to an armed uprising and even revolution.

KEY IDEAS

- Dissatisfaction with unions led to support for the Chartists

- The Chartist petitions failed

- Some Chartists used violence

- Most aims were granted eventually

SOURCE 6
An artist's view of the Chartist riot at Newport, 1839. ▼

Petitions were presented to Parliament in 1839, 1842 and 1848. On each occasion they were rejected, and this led to riots. In 1839 there were riots in Birmingham and Newport, Monmouthshire. A large Chartist mob, led by John Frost, attacked Newport's Westgate Hotel, in an attempt to free a number of Chartists held prisoner there. They were driven back by troops, leaving fourteen dead. Several Chartists, including Frost, were sentenced to imprisonment or transportation.

SOURCE 7

A description of the rising by a modern historian:

At nine o'clock in the morning of the 4th November 1839 the Chartists arrived in Newport armed with old muskets, pikes and clubs. Police and special constables were waiting for them, but retreated into the Westgate Hotel. The Chartist leader marched across the square with the intention of speaking to the Mayor, when, from the windows of the hotel, the police opened fire. For about twenty minutes the chartists were trapped by which time fourteen of their number lay dead and about fifty wounded, of whom ten died later. Then the rest fled.

The rejection of the 1842 petition sparked the 'plug' riots in Lancashire. Rioters went round the factories removing the plugs from the boilers to stop the factories working.

The petition of 1848 marked the final failure of the movement. This petition was said to contain 5 million signatures, but actually had only 2 million. A mass meeting held on Kennington Common, London, was to be followed by a march on Parliament. The marchers were turned back by 150,000 special constables.

SOURCE 8

From the Mayor of Newport's account of the Rising:

I collected together 500 honest men and swore them in as special constables. I also sent 30 soldiers to defend the Westgate Hotel in which a number of Chartists were being held prisoner. The Chartists entered the town and stopped outside the hotel. Six of them entered and one of them opened fire on a constable. The order was given for the soldiers to open fire. The shutters of the hotel were flung back and the soldiers fired three volleys into the mob.

What were the reasons for failure?

● Many left rather than support a policy of physical force.
● Leadership was generally poor.
● The firm measures of the Government discouraged many from joining.
● In the late 1840s increased prosperity brought more jobs.
● Many followed other causes such as the Anti-Corn Law League and the Ten Hours Movement.
● Many of the signatures on the petitions were proved to be forgeries.

Were the Chartists' six points ever achieved?

● Acts in 1867, 1884 and 1918 gradually extended the vote to all adult males.
● A redistribution of constituencies gave a more equal electorate in the years after 1885.
● The property qualification to become an MP was removed in 1858.
● In 1872 secret ballots were introduced.
● Under an Act of 1911, MPs were to be paid.
● Annual Parliaments are impractical although, under an Act passed in 1911, the life of a Parliament is limited to five years.

Questions

1. Explain why working class people had found it difficult to organise in the early 19th century (see pages 144-147).

2. What were the aims of the Chartists?

3. Why did so many want to join the movement?

4. Look at Source 6. How accurate an interpretation is this source?

5. Sources 7 and 8 give different versions of the Newport Rising.
   (a) How do they differ?
   (b) Why do they differ?
   (c) Does the fact that they differ mean they are of no use to a historian studying the Newport Rising?

5. 'In the short-term, Chartism had failed. Yet the ideas of the movement lived on.' How far would you agree with this statement?

14.3 *How successful was 'New Unionism'*

New Model Unions

Most of the unions before 1870 were for skilled, or semi-skilled, workers. These were the craft, or 'new model' unions, for workers, whose jobs required a long period of training, such as carpenters and engineers. The first of these unions was the **Amalgamated Society of Engineers**, set up in 1851. Similar unions of carpenters, bricklayers and iron-founders were formed. These unions were characterised by:
• charging members high subscriptions of 1s (5p) per week;
• giving members unemployment and sickness pay, an old-age pension and death benefits;
• being well organised, with paid officials working from a permanent headquarters;
• aiming to improve members' wages and conditions of work by negotiation rather than strikes.

KEY IDEAS

• The working class needed representation

• Trade unions gained increased power

• Growth of the Labour Party

Because of their moderation these unions helped made trade unions acceptable. In 1860 the London Trades Council (called the 'Junta'), was set up to campaign to improve the legal position of trade unions. This was made up of the secretaries of the new model unions. In 1868, 34 trade union delegates met at a 'Congress' in Manchester and the Trades Union Congress (TUC) became accepted as the central organisation for trade unions.

SOURCE 9

From the memoirs of Joseph Arch, founder of the NALU, 1898:

After the harvest of 1871 had been reaped and the winter had set in the sufferings of the men became cruel and by 1872 there seemed to be two doors open to them. One door led to a life of degradation in the workhouse; the other to the grave. Their poverty had fallen to starvation point and was past all bearing. They saw that if they were to rise out of their miserable state, they must force open a door of escape for themselves. Oppression and hunger and misery made them desperate, and desperation was the mother of the union.

New Unionism

The 1870s and 1880s saw the growth of unions for unskilled workers. These 'New Unions':
- were for the lower-paid and often unskilled workers;
- had low subscriptions that their members could afford, but did not pay out benefits, such as sick pay;
- were more militant, meaning they were more ready to strike, than earlier unions;
- concentrated on shortening working hours and increasing wages.

These unions grew because:
- There was an increase in the number of unskilled workers due to the technical changes in industry and transport.
- Unskilled workers were receiving higher wages giving them a greater sense of independence and power.
- A number of strong-willed and determined union leaders emerged.
- Unskilled workers were more aware of their rights through increased education.
- During the 1870s there was a trade depression in industry and agriculture. Many workers felt that trade unions were one way of fighting high unemployment and low wages.
- As trade improved, the workers realised that union membership put them in a stronger position.

The coal miners were the first unskilled workers to form a union to improve safety, and to bring about a fairer system of payment for work. In 1872 the National Miners Association forced

◄ **SOURCE 10**
Procession of match girls to the Houses of Parliament, 1888. A contemporary print.

SOURCE 11

Annie Besant's description of 'phossy-jaw':

Emma Harris had pain in her upper and lower jaws. Her throat glands were swollen and painful, her gums were inflamed. Her teeth became loose and started to fall out. She was operated on twice. Fear prevented her from going back to hospital to have a third operation to get a false jaw and teeth put in.

the Government to introduce a law to ensure that all mines were tested for safety every day. In 1887 the miners introduced a system to ensure that they were paid the correct amount.

In 1872 the **National Agricultural Labourers' Union (NALU)** was founded. Very quickly it had 100,000 members. Most landowners and farmers were against the idea of the union and they organised a lock-out in 1874. As many labourers lived in tied-cottages that came with their jobs, they could be thrown out of their homes if they were sacked. Many went on strike against the lock-outs and evictions, but, after a few months of hardship, the farm-workers gave up the struggle and the NALU collapsed.

The match girls

In 1888 Annie Besant, a journalist, discovered that match girls had to work standing up for as long as 11 hours a day. The typical wage of a match girl was 4s (20p) a week. The girls were in danger of contracting 'phossy jaw'. This is a form of gangrene (decay) caused by the phosphorous used to make the matches (see Source 11).

Annie Besant wrote a newspaper article describing the match girls' working conditions. She called upon people to stop buying Bryant and May matches until the employers agreed to improve conditions. To force the issue, 1,400 match girls went on strike (Source 10). Public opinion was on the side of the match girls, and their strike was successful. This was the first success of new unionism.

The gas workers

The unskilled men at the London Gas Light and Coke Company, led by William Thorne, threatened a strike in 1889. This threat was enough to reduce the working day from 12 to 8 hours without a reduction in pay.

The London Dockers Strike, 1889

Dockers in London were paid wages as low as 5d (2p) an hour. Often they were only taken on for an hour at a time, depending on the number of ships in port. These largely unskilled workers were starving. Ben Tillett, leader of the General Labourers Union, organised a campaign to gain improved conditions for the dockers. He demanded a pay increase to 6d ($2^1/_2$p) an hour (the 'docker's tanner'), with a guaranteed minimum of four hours work. The employers refused, and the dockers went on strike. The strike spread to the whole of the Port of London.

The strikers picketed the docks, allowing no strike-breakers through. They organised large, orderly marches through London to collect funds and raise support. Soon the port was at a standstill, with food rotting on the ships. When it looked as though the dockers might have to give in, they were saved by an unexpected donation of £30,000 from Australian trade unions.

After five weeks, the dock owners were persuaded to listen to the advice of the mediating committee, which included the Catholic Cardinal Manning, and the dockers won.

These strikes brought about great changes in Britain's trade unions. Thousands of unskilled workers began to organise themselves into large unions based on a whole industry, rather than on a skilled craft within an industry. Examples included the General Railway Workers Union, and a Miners Federation of Great Britain. Even the NALU was revived. The total membership of the trade union movement doubled.

Despite this, the employers often held the upper hand because, when unemployment was high, workers tended to leave their unions – because either they were unemployed or they were frightened of losing their jobs.

As economic conditions became worse in the 1890s the gas workers' and dockers' unions collapsed, and the NALU folded. Despite these setbacks, trade unions were now an essential part of Britain's economic and political life.

SOURCE 12
Engaging dock labourers at the West India Dock.
◄

SOURCE 13 *A procession of London dockers through the streets of the city.* ▲

The growth of the Labour Party

Gradually the working class realised they could not depend on the Liberal or Conservative Parties for serious support. A link was needed between socialists, and the growing trade union movement with its large funds and mass support.

The man who achieved this was James Keir Hardie. He was a Scottish miner who first stood for Parliament in 1888. He was annoyed with the way he was treated by the Liberal Party and so, with the help of others, founded the Scottish Labour Party in 1888. In 1892 he stood again for Parliament, and was elected as an independent socialist. In 1893 the Independent Labour Party was set up. In 1906, 29 Labour MPs were elected. The Labour Party grew very slowly, but it was helped by MPs being awarded a salary of £400 per year in 1911. By 1918 it held 57 seats. The Labour Party was becoming a formidable force. After 1911 the party even had its own newspaper, the *Daily Herald*.

Questions

1. Why did trade unions for unskilled workers grow?

2. The reasons listed below state why it was more difficult for unskilled workers to form trade unions. Place them in order of importance and explain why you selected this order.
   (a) Unskilled workers were paid less than skilled workers.
   (b) Unskilled workers did not have the vote.
   (c) Unskilled workers were easier to replace than skilled workers.
   (d) Unskilled workers were less well educated.
   (e) There was little public support for unskilled workers.

3. How did 'new unionism' differ from the New Model Unions?

4. Why do you think the match girls were successful in their strike?

5. Was the Dockers Strike successful?

How successful were courts and Parliament in curbing the power of the unions?

In the second half of the 19th century, and the early years of the 20th century, the unions were affected in different ways by legislation and the courts of law.

Hornby v Close, 1867

The judgment relating to this case refused the Bradford branch of the Boilermakers' Society permission to prosecute their treasurer for stealing the funds. This judgment meant that, if union funds were stolen by a union official, unions were unable to take legal action against the thief to recover the money.

Trade Union Act, 1871

Under this Act, trade unions became full legal organisations. As a result, their funds were legally protected from theft by officials.

Criminal Law Amendment Act, 1871

This Act prohibited picketing. This weakened the strike weapon, and angered trade

SOURCE 14 ▲
Photograph of the cheque paid to Taff Vale Railway Company, 1901.

unionists. Under this Act, gas workers received harsh prison sentences in 1872. Later, 12 women farm workers were imprisoned for intimidating strike breakers.

In the 1874 general election many trade unionists voted for the Conservatives against the Liberals who had passed the Act.

SOURCE 15 *Unions' legal rights 1867-1913.* ▼

| **1867 Hornby v Close** – unions unable to take legal action if funds stolen by a union official | **1871 Trade Union Act** – trade unions become legal organisations. Able to take action if funds stolen by official
Criminal Law Amendment Act – picketing prohibited | **1875 Conspiracy and Protection of Property Act** – trade unions allowed to use peaceful picketing | **1901 Taff Vale Judgment** – unions liable for employers' financial losses during strikes |

Year	Number of unions	Number of members	Number of strikes
1900	1,323	2,022,000	633
1902	1,297	2,013,000	432
1904	1,256	1,967,000	346
1906	1,282	2,210,000	479
1908	1,268	2,415,000	389
1910	1,269	2,565,000	521
1912	1,252	3,416,000	834
1914	1,260	4,145,000	973

SOURCE 16 ▲
Trade unions: membership and strikes, 1900-1914.

Conspiracy and Protection of Property Act, 1875

This Act was passed by the Conservative Government. It permitted trade unions to use peaceful picketing during strikes.

The legislation of the 1870s established the power of the trade unions. They could now organise effective strikes if peaceful bargaining failed. In the period 1900-1914 trade union membership grew to over 4 million (Source 16). During this period their power was challenged by two court decisions.

The Taff Vale Judgment, 1901

In 1900 there was a strike on the Taff Vale railway in South Wales. The manager of the railway company brought a court action against the workers' union, the Amalgamated Society of Railway Servants. He claimed damages for the loss that the railway company had suffered because of the strike. The case went to the House of Lords. In 1902 the company was awarded £23,000 damages and costs against the union (Source 14).

As this judgment would apply to all future cases, it made strikes almost impossible. In 1906 the new Liberal Government introduced a **Trades Dispute Act**. The main clause in this Act was that unions were not liable for losses caused by strike action.

The Osborne Judgment, 1909

W. V. Osborne was a member of the Amalgamated Society of Railway Servants. He supported the Liberal Party, so he objected to the union giving part of his union subscription, the 'political levy', to the Labour Party and brought an action against his union to stop them doing this.

The case went to the House of Lords which decided that the political levy was illegal. This was a severe blow to the Labour Party because union money was used to support Labour MPs in Parliament.

In 1913, the Government passed the Trade Union Act, 1913. This said that the political levy was legal – provided that a majority of the union's members voted for it. Anyone who did not want to pay could 'contract out', that is, not pay.

The period 1900-1914 was a period of increasing conflict between employers and the unions. The worst incidents were in the coal and shipbuilding industries. At the time it was the view of many people that the unions were becoming too powerful. On the other hand, unionists would have argued that it was the fault of the Government and employers who kept wages down. A crisis was only prevented by the outbreak of war in 1914. However, the underlying issues still remained and surfaced again after the end of the war.

1906 Trades Dispute Act – unions not liable for employers' losses due to strike action

1909 Osborne Judgment – political levy illegal

1913 Trade Union Act – political levy legal, but union members could 'contract out'

Questions

1. Describe the attempts to curb the power of the unions in the period up to 1914.

2. How successful were these actions?

3. Why was the payment of the cheque (Source 14) an important event in trade union history?

4. How true is it to say that 'the unions made little progress in the period 1870 to 1914'? Explain your answer.

14.5 *The General Strike*

Coal mines had been nationalised during the First World War. In 1921 they returned to private ownership. The owners immediately decided to make wage cuts. The miners refused to accept these cuts and asked the Triple Alliance of Miners, Transport Workers and Railwaymen for help. A huge strike was planned for 15 April 1921, but at the last moment the miners were left on their own. The 15th April became known as 'Black Friday'. After three months on strike, the miners had to return to work on the owners' terms. Further pay cuts were proposed in early 1926, following a decline in trade. The miners' spokesman, A. J. Cooke demanded, *'Not a penny off the pay, not a minute on the day!'*. On Tuesday 4 May 1926 the **General Strike** started.

SOURCE 17
Waterloo Station, London, showing the rush hour on the first day of the strike.

THE BEGINNING

SOURCE 18
A convoy of lorries driven by volunteers and protected by an armoured vehicle and soldiers, leaving London Docks on 7 May.

READY …

... FOR ACTION

SOURCE 19
An account by a person who was present during the strike:
▼

One morning we heard troops were unloading ships and that lorries were coming up the Victoria Dock Road manned by troops. Sure enough, when we got to Barking Road up came the lorries with barbed wire all round their canopies and troops with guns sitting behind the barbed wire. The people were jeering and booing, but that was the extent of their reactions. It was quite good-humoured. Then the police started pushing from behind and they kept pushing us into the road. This led to arguments and before we knew it the police were laying about us with truncheons. That caused more anger. There was a real explosion for about half an hour.

Questions

1. What can you learn about the General Strike from Source 17?

2. Study Sources 18, 19 and 20. Which of these sources agree the most? Explain your answer with reference to all three sources.

3. Study Source 21. This source is written by somebody who was involved in the strike. Does this mean it must be more reliable than any of the other sources? Explain your answer using the source and your own knowledge.

4. Study Sources 20 and 21. These sources give different versions of the success of the strike.
(a) What reasons can you give for this?
(b) Does the fact that they differ mean they are of no use to a historian studying the General Strike?
Explain your answers using the sources and your own knowledge.

5. 'There were winners and losers in the General Strike.' Using the sources and your own knowledge, explain whether or not you agree with this statement.

ORDER AND QUIET THROUGH THE LAND.

Growing Dissatisfaction Among The Strikers.

INCREASING NUMBERS OF MEN RETURNING TO WORK.

850 Omnibuses In The Streets Of London.

MORE AND MORE TRAINS.

SOURCE 20 ▲
From the front page of the British Gazette, *May 12 1926.*

SOURCE 21 ▼
Memories of a miner who helped to organise the strike in South Wales:

With the ending of the General Strike and the miners refusing to go back to work, it was generally understood that they should try to wear us down. A phrase was used that the battle would be fought on the empty stomachs of the wives and children. The distress in the mining valleys was acute. My wife remembers seeing a number of boys wearing potato sacks cut into trousers.

THE END

14.6 *How did the General Strike affect trade unions*

The TUC called off the General Strike after nine days. The miners struggled on alone for six months, until poverty and hunger forced them to accept lower wages and longer hours. The Strike failed because the Government was able to win over public support and keep essential services going. The TUC was not well prepared, and the Labour Party was divided.

SOURCE 22
Size and number of unions 1900-1950.

The effects of the General Strike

Its failure was a blow to the trade union movement:
- union membership fell;
- the Government passed the **Trades Disputes Act** in 1927, making general and sympathy strikes illegal;
- many overseas coal markets were lost;
- trade unions became unpopular with the public.

	No. of Unions	No. of members (in 000s)		
		Men	Women	Total
1900	1,323	1,808	154	2,022
1910	1,269	2,287	278	2,565
1920	1,384	7,006	1,343	8,348
1930	1,121	4,049	793	4,842
1945	781	6,237	1,638	7,875
1950	732	7,605	1,684	9,289

Years of decline

The years after 1927 were difficult for trade unions. Unemployment remained high in the 1930s, but morale among trade union members was low. There were few strikes.

SOURCE 23

In a 1926 speech by Ernest Bevin said:

The General Strike is a weapon that cannot be used for industrial purposes. It is clumsy and not very effective. It has no goal. Some people will blame the TUC for the failure of the strike, some will blame the miners. But the real blame is with the General Strike itself and those who preached it without thinking about it.

Moderate leaders, such as Ernest Bevin, tried to improve relationships with both Government and the public.

Post-war changes

Union membership began to flourish after the Second World War, and by 1980 about half of the workforce belonged to a trade union. The growth was mainly due to white-collared women workers, such as local government officers and hospital staff, joining unions. The number of unions began to fall as smaller groups amalgamated to form more powerful, larger unions.

*Q*uestion

Describe how trade unions were affected by the General Strike.

14.7 *How powerful are unions today* ?

The 1950s and 1960s

During this period, the Conservative Governments tried to limit wage increases by introducing '**wage freezes**'. The number of strikes increased. Many of these strikes were unofficial '**wildcat**' strikes. Small groups of workers, particularly in the car industry, held '**lightening**' **strikes** which halted production. In addition, there were a number of demarcation disputes (about who did what job). The '**closed shop**' system, which restricted employment in certain industries to trade union members only, was also criticised.

Harold Wilson, Labour Prime Minister from 1964, tried to improve relations between unions and employers. In 1969 he, together with his Secretary for Employment, Barbara Castle, produced a plan called '**In Place of Strife**'. This was designed to restrict unofficial

> ### KEY IDEAS
> - 'Winter of Discontent' led to anti-union feeling
> - Conflict with Government
> - Laws reduced effectiveness

strikes by requiring a ballot before strike action was taken, and a 28 day 'cooling off' period before workers took industrial action. It was disliked by most trade unions and, as they funded the Labour Party, Wilson had to withdraw his plan.

SOURCE 24
Miners marching through Mansfield, at the end of the strike, 1974. ▼

The 1970s and 1980s

The Conservative Government, led by Edward Heath, introduced an **Industrial Relations Act** in 1971. This Act:

- made ballots compulsory before all strikes;
- banned 'closed shop' arrangements;
- set up the National Industrial Relations Court to settle disputes;
- gave the power to fine or imprison those who ignored it.

But the majority of unions refused to co-operate, and the Act was soon challenged. Heath became involved in a dispute with the miners in January 1972. The National Coal Board offered the miners an 8% pay rise. The miners wanted double this, and went on strike. The miners' strike was led by Arthur Scargill who introduced the idea of **'flying pickets'** to prevent the movement of coal to the power stations. After six weeks the miners won an average increase of 21%.

In June 1972 the dockers came out on strike, after their union was fined £55,000 for contempt of court. The railwaymen also went on strike at this time. A 14% wage increase was granted, and the 1971 Act was effectively dead.

In November 1973, the miners refused a pay increase of 16% and introduced an overtime ban. About the same time, a massive energy crisis hit the country, as supplies of oil went down drastically because of disputes in the Middle East. From January 1974 a three-day week was introduced. Display lighting and advertising was banned. Television transmission ended at 10.30 pm. Regular power cuts meant spending every other night without electricity. On 5 February the miners went on strike. A general election was called, partly on the issue of 'who should govern the country' – the Government or the unions. The Conservatives were defeated and the Labour Party returned to power. They immediately settled the miners' strike (see Source 23).

Labour abolished the Industrial Relations Act and introduced a **'Social Contract'**. Under this contract, the Government and the unions were to negotiate a fair pay increase each year. In return, the Government agreed to increase pensions, state benefits and child allowances. The Social Contract did not work well, as the Government was unable to keep prices down. In January and February 1979, there were strikes by ambulance drivers, health workers, teachers and local government workers. This caused much anti-union feeling, especially as the hospital workers' strikes led to longer

---

1980   *EMPLOYMENT ACT*

- Restricted the use of 'flying pickets' (union members who travel from place to place to take part in picketing and strike action).
- Gave legal protection to those workers who did not wish to join a union.
- Made funds available for secret ballots.

1982   *EMPLOYMENT ACT*

- Made it illegal to dismiss a worker for not belonging to a union.

1984   *TRADE UNION ACT*

- Unions to hold secret ballots before all strikes.
- Ballots to be held regularly to see whether union members wanted to have a political fund (to pay money to the Labour Party).
- Elections of trade union officials to be held every five years.

SOURCE 25
The Conservatives and trade unions, 1980–1984. ▲

▲ SOURCE 26
*Leyland workers marching in protest
at the Social Contract, 1977.*

waiting lists. As a result of this 'Winter of
Discontent', James Callaghan, the Labour
Prime Minister, called a general election.
The Conservatives, under Margaret Thatcher,
were returned to power, by promising to
carry out major trade union reform (see
Source 25).

In 1984-85 there was another miners'
strike, this time over pit closures. The miners
picketed ports and coal-mines. The tactics
used in the 1970s failed. Coal was no longer
a key industry. Many miners refused to strike.
The police were deployed in large numbers
and reduced the threat of flying pickets,
making sure imported supplies were kept up.
The winter was mild which reduced demand
for coal. The Conservative Government was
determined to win at all costs and, after over
a year on strike, the miners returned to work.
Few of their demands had been met.

Despite their difficulties, trade unions are
now well established with millions of
members relying on them for a range of
benefits. They have retained their strength

in the public sector, but this sector is less
important today because many of the major
nationalised industries have been privatised.
In the private sector, where increasingly no-
strike agreements have been agreed, unions are
less strong. A House of Commons committee
reported in 1994 that '*trade unions need to
make more effort to adapt to the needs of the
private sector*'.

Questions

1. Describe the agreement of 1974 called
   the 'Social Contract'.

2. What was the 'Winter of Discontent'?

3. In what ways were people affected
   by the miners' strikes of the 1970s?

4. Could it be said that Governments have
   been successful in curbing the power of
   the unions in the years since 1960?

15 EDUCATION

15.1 *Was educational provision before 1830 adequate* ?

At the beginning of the 19th century there was no state-run education system. All schools were run privately, either by individuals or by voluntary bodies, such as churches. It was up to parents to arrange and pay for any schooling their children had. Most children, especially those of poor parents, received little or no schooling.

Education for the poor

Dame schools were small schools each run by an old lady. They provided little more than a place for young children to be left while parents went out to work. The rooms were often crowded, and education was limited to sewing, knitting and reading the Bible. Fees had to be paid, but these were small. A Government enquiry in 1818 recorded that there were 3,000 of these schools. A report about Manchester in 1834 said that in one dame school were '*31 children from 2 to 7 years of age. The room was a cellar about 10 feet square and about 7 feet high*'.

Charity schools were run by religious charities, such as the Society for the Propagation of Christian Knowledge (SPCK) which had been founded in 1699. The society was funded by public donation, so it had no regular or reliable income. However, by 1730 it was operating over 1,500 schools. Through these schools it was hoped that poor children would learn obedience and to accept their place in society. Education was often of a low standard, and was mainly reading, writing, arithmetic and memorising the Bible.

Many poor children were child workers who received no schooling at all. Robert Raikes, a newspaper editor, believed that for children to become law-abiding adults it was important that they were taught Christian principles. As Sunday was working children's only free day, he decided to open a **Sunday School**. His first school opened in Gloucester in 1780 (Source 2). The original aim was to teach reading, so that children could grow up able to read the Bible for themselves, but writing and arithmetic were taught as well. The Sunday School movement spread rapidly, encouraged by the Methodist church, the Church of England and some factory owners. The Sunday Schools were mainly funded by voluntary subscriptions.

Ragged schools were set up by individuals as acts of charity for the poorest of children (See Source 1). The pupils would not have been allowed to attend other voluntary schools because *'their ragged, diseased and crime-worn appearance would scare away the children of better off parents'*. It was the children's only hope of any education. In 1844, Lord Shaftesbury founded the Ragged Schools' Union to help with fund-raising for these schools.

SOURCE 1

A ragged school for the very poor and homeless. ▲

▶ **KEY IDEAS**

- Schools were provided by voluntary bodies not the state

- Many children did not attend school

- Fees for attendance were paid

- Change was needed after the Industrial Revolution

SOURCE 2

This description of the benefits of Sunday schools appeared in the Gloucester Journal, *3 November 1783:*

Inhabitants of the towns and villages, complain that they receive more injury to their property on the Sabbath than during the rest of the week. This is because of the lawless state of the young who are allowed to run wild on that day, free from every restraint. To remedy this evil, they attend Sunday School thus keeping their minds engaged. In the parishes where the plan has been adopted, we are assured that the behaviour of the children is greatly civilised.

Tom Brown's Schooldays *a novel by Thomas Hughes, written in 1857, gives this description of discipline at Rugby School:*

Dr Arnold, the headmaster states after prayers in the morning that no boy is to go down into the town. Wherefore East and Tom, for no earthly pleasure except that of doing what they are told not to do, straight away, after second lesson go down into town and run plump into one of the masters as they emerge into the High Street. He sends East and Tom up to the Doctor who on learning they had been at prayers that morning, flogs them soundly. They have each been flogged several times recently for direct and wilful breaches of rules.

Education for the better-off

Girls from more well-to-do families were often taught at home by a **governess**. They were taught reading, writing, music, painting and dancing. Mothers often assisted, particularly in the teaching of sewing, cookery and the management of household accounts. At girls' private **boarding schools** lessons also concentrated on good manners and behaviour – the skills girls needed to attract husbands and to be good wives.

Most towns had a **grammar school**. Many had been founded in Tudor times to teach the classics (Latin and Greek) to local boys. During the 18th century demand increased for a wider variety of subjects to meet the needs of the Industrial Revolution. The grammar schools' charters did not allow them to change what they taught, so their curriculum became out-of-date. Few parents chose to send their sons to these schools, and the standard of teaching fell.

Many of the **public schools** had been established in the later middle ages. Among the most famous were Eton, Rugby, Winchester and Harrow. These schools were attended by the sons of the upper class and nobility, and by sons of some merchants and industrialists. Many pupils were sent far from home to public schools. Public schools attracted more pupils than grammar schools. However, many of the teachers were Church of England clergymen, and the curriculum was similar to grammar schools, so they did not really educate boys for careers in industrial Britain. School discipline was often brutal (Source 3) and conditions harsh. Bullying was common and a system of 'fagging' operated, where younger boys acted as servants to the older pupils.

Dissenting academies were run by non-conformists and were often the best type of school. These were schools for girls as well as for boys. Their curriculum included science and maths, and the teaching was good.

Private schools were mainly attended by children from the middle classes. These included girls' boarding schools. Many private schools were badly run, with poorly-educated teachers. Many of them had a reputation for neglecting their pupils. Charles Dickens described life at this kind of school in *Nicholas Nickleby* (1838). He based his fictional Dotheboys Hall, and its cruel headmaster Mr Squeers, on the case of the real Bowes Academy in Yorkshire. At that school, while a Mr Shaw was headmaster, twenty-five boys died of starvation, disease and neglect.

The developing Britain of the Industrial Revolution demanded changes in the education of Britain's children. There was a demand for improved scientific and technical training, to produce skilled workers, engineers, and other professionals, to meet the requirements of the new 'mechanical age'.

SOURCE 5

A.D. Coleridge, writing in 1885, remembers his school days at Eton in the 1840s:

I say nothing of having one's nightcap set on fire in the night or having one's bed turned on end and finding one's heels in the air. The rioting and drinking that took place after the doors were closed can scarcely be credited. My dinner consisted of excellent bread but most of it was wasted as the elder boys used to pelt each other with it.

◀ **SOURCE 4**
Eton College in 1816.

The rapid growth of population, and the movement of people from the countryside to the towns, meant there was a serious shortage of schools in some of the industrial areas. So, despite voluntary schools, most children from poor families did not receive any kind of education even in the first quarter of the 19th century. Major changes needed to take place to produce a system of education which was adequate for a rising industrial society.

15.2 *How successful was the monitorial system* ?

The monitorial system of teaching was used in schools run by two voluntary societies. These societies wanted to provide education for children living in the industrial towns. They did a great deal for the provision of elementary schools, and also for teacher training. Pupils attending the schools had to pay a small fee. Other funds came from church collections and voluntary subscriptions.

The British and Foreign Schools Society was founded in 1808 by Joseph Lancaster, a Quaker. Supported by non-conformists, this Society built and ran schools offering elementary education (the '3Rs' – reading, writing and arithmetic – and scripture). 'Lancasterian Schools' were built all over Britain.

SOURCE 6

Andrew Bell commented on the monitorial system in 1807:

It is not proposed that the children of the poor be educated in an expensive manner, or even taught to write and do arithmetic. There is a risk of elevating them from their drudgery of daily labour above their condition, and thereby making them discontented and unhappy in their lot. It may be enough to teach most children to read their Bible.

KEY IDEAS

- Facts were learned by rote
- Large numbers received a basic education

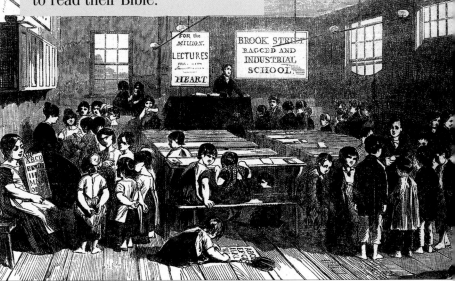

SOURCE 7
A school using the monitorial system. ▶

SOURCE 8

In 1902 an eighty-year-old man had this memory of his school days under the monitorial system:

In the front row the Monitor held a board on which was plainly printed the capitals and small letters of the alphabet. My little teacher pointed to a letter and shouted its name, which we repeated aloud. He then told us to smooth the sand in front of us, and try to make the letter by marking the sand. After this was done, we again shouted the letter.

The National Society was founded by Dr Andrew Bell, in 1811, to provide schools based on the religious teaching of the Church of England.

Lancaster and Bell introduced their own educational ideas into these schools. They both claimed to have developed the '**monitorial system**' of teaching. This meant that one teacher could 'teach' several

SOURCE 9

The inscription stones of many National Schools have survived. A look in your own area might reveal examples like this one: ▼

SOURCE 10

A modern historian commented on the monitorial system:

The monitorial system was in many ways a successful one. Schools of two or three hundred could be run by a single teacher at very little cost, because the monitors cost next to nothing to employ. To some extent, these schools resembled a factory. The children were like raw material. They would all be made into identical products, filled with some information and ideas.

hundred children. This made education cheaper. It also meant, however, that the only kind of study was learning by memory (also called learning 'by rote').

Under the monitorial system the teacher taught the older pupils (monitors) who then instructed the younger children. The younger children usually repeated what they were being taught several times, and wrote it on a slate. All pupils learnt basic facts at the same speed through parrot-like repetition. There was no opportunity to ask questions. Often, neither the monitors nor the younger children understood what they were repeating. Discipline, because of the large numbers, was strict.

SOURCE 11

A Government inspector had this to say after an inspection in 1840:

Thirty-one girls read Mark Chapter 12 from the Bible to the monitor. The noise in the school was so great that as I sat by the monitor I could not hear the girl who was reading in the class. Several children were laughing to each other, others were inattentive. The mistress was occupied in another part of the school.

Questions

1. Look at Source 7. What does this source tell you about how the monitorial system worked?

2. Look at Sources 7 and 8. How different were monitorial schools to the dame schools you read about on page 162?

3. Look at Source 9. How can remains like this help us to develop our understanding of education?

4. (a) Look at Sources 10 and 11. These sources give different versions of the monitorial system. What reasons can you give to explain this?

   (b) Does the fact that these sources differ mean they are of no use to a historian studying the monitorial system?

6. Read Source 8. This source is the only one from somebody who was taught in a monitorial school. Does this mean it must be more reliable than any of the other sources? Explain your answer.

7. Did the monitorial system bring an improvement to education for the poor? Use this section and pages 163–165 to help you answer this question.

15.3 *Why and how did the state begin to take an interest in education*?

During the early 19th century, the numbers of children to be educated rose. Not only was the population increasing, but in 1833 the first Act was passed for compulsory education for some children. The 1833 Factory Act required children working in cotton mills to receive two hours schooling per day – this was increased to three hours in 1844. As the 19th century went on, it became clear that the voluntary societies could not cope with educating the increasing number of children. It seemed as if the government would have to be involved in providing **elementary (basic) education**. As the Industrial Revolution continued to create new jobs, it was obvious that higher standards of education were needed for the workers. However, there was opposition to the idea of elementary education for all.

KEY IDEAS

- Changing industry required widespread education
- Government became involved from 1833
- Education was either cheap or efficient

Arguments for Government involvement in elementary education:

- Schooling was necessary to create an improved workforce.
- As the working-class became more politically powerful, it was important to retain social stability by making the population more responsible through education.
- The voluntary societies did not have the resources to keep up with the demand for more schools, and so needed Government help.
- The decline of the Church meant that more schools were needed for religious education.

SOURCE 12

Matthew Arnold, a Government inspector, made this comment in his general report of 1869:

It is found possible to get children through the Revised Code examination without their really knowing how to read, write and do arithmetic. A book is selected at the beginning of the year for the children of a certain standard; all the year the children read this book over and over again, and no other. When the inspector comes they are presented to read this book; they can read their sentence or two fluently enough, but cannot read any other book fluently. Yet the letter of the law is satisfied.

SOURCE 13

An old man remembered his schooldays in the 1860s:

Two inspectors came once a year and carried out a dramatic examination. Each would sit at a desk and children would be called in turn to one or the other. The master stood near by and the children could see him looking cross as a good pupil stuck at a word in the reading book or sat motionless with his sum in front of him. The master's anxiety was deep as his earnings depended on the children's work.

◀ **SOURCE 14**
An artist's impression of a school inspector testing pupils in the 1860s.

Arguments against Government involvement in elementary education:

● Government should not interfere in the provision of education because it was not the role of the state to interfere in the lives of the people.
● Schools could give people ideas above their social station in life, and so make them politically dangerous.

In 1833 the Government gave direct help to education for the first time. An annual grant of £20,000 was made to be shared between the National Society and the British and Foreign Society. Though small, this grant indicated that the Government had accepted that education was one of its responsibilities. The grant was increased to £30,000 in 1839 and in that year the government set up a committee to look at how the money was being spent. To do this they appointed a

number of school inspectors. By 1860 the grant had reached £500,000 per year.

The Government also became involved in teacher training through the pupil-teacher system. Under this system, selected older children stayed on at school to receive extra tuition. They could also apply for a scholarship to go to a teacher training college. The first college was opened in 1840 in Battersea by James Kay-Shuttleworth. In the 1850s there were more than 10,000 pupil-teachers and they quickly replaced the monitors.

Because the amount of public money involved in education was becoming so large, the Government appointed a Royal Commission in 1858 under the chairmanship of the Duke of Newcastle. The Commission was set up to enquire into the state of elementary education in England and Wales, with a view to providing '*an extension of sound and cheap education to all classes*'.

The Newcastle Commission reported its findings in 1861. It revealed that, although most children now received some education, great ignorance still existed among schoolchildren, especially in the industrial areas. It stated that schools were badly run, often had poor quality teachers, and were overcrowded.

SOURCE 15

These are some memories of Charles Cooper, who went to school in the 1870s:

In those days the amount of Government grant paid to a school depended on the achievements of all its scholars in the 3Rs in an examination carried out by Her Majesty's Inspectors. Of course, the Headmaster's ideal was to get 100% passes, and then his school would get the highest grant. Hence every effort was made to get every child passed in all three subjects. It was a cruel system. The cane was used freely for both boys and girls. The idea was that every child could do the work if he tried hard enough, and he was made to try by the threat of punishment.

The Government attempted to improve matters through the Revised Code of 1862 which introduced 'payment by results'. As the minister for education, Robert Lowe, put it, *'If [education] is not cheap, it shall be efficient. If it is not efficient, it shall be cheap'.* Government grants were now to be made on the basis of:

- annual inspection of the school;
- pupils' attendance rates;
- pupils' performance based on results of tests on the '3Rs' (reading, writing and arithmetic) carried out by the Inspectors of Schools.

Each pupil could earn for the school a maximum of 12s (60p) by their performance and attendance.

The system was far from perfect. It had a harmful effect on teaching, as pupils were drilled over and over again on the tests. This encouraged parrot-like repetition of spellings and tables. Pupils memorised but did not understand. Some inspectors reported that pupils read the test passages while holding the book upside-down!

The slow learners often received severe punishments to 'encourage' their learning, while the more able were often ignored.

Schools in poorer districts were penalised, because attendance in these areas was usually worse than the better-off areas.

As teachers' salaries depended on the grant, they sometimes tried to cheat the inspector. For example, some teachers stood behind the inspector during the test mouthing the correct answer to the pupil.

Though it was criticised, this system existed until 1897. However, the changes had not solved the shortage of schools. Some people believed that it was the responsibility of the Government to ensure that the gaps were filled.

National Schoolmaster (going round with Government Inspector),
"Wilkins, how do you bring shillings into pence?"
Pupil, "I takes it round to the Public House, sir!"

◀ **SOURCE 16**
This cartoon from Punch *shows little respect for testing in schools.*

Questions

1. What reasons can you give for the Government becoming involved in education?

2. Why was the Newcastle Commission set up?

3. How did the Revised Code attempt to improve schools? Do you think it was successful?

4. Describe the visit of an inspector to a school.

5. How useful were Sources 14 and 16 in helping you answer question 4?

15.4 Did the 1870 Act create a state system of elementary education?

In the 1860s there was growing pressure for state action to improve education:

● The 1867 Reform Act had given the vote to many working men in the towns. It was then thought that they should have some schooling to be able to vote responsibly. The education minister, Robert Lowe said, *'Now we must educate our masters'*.

● Trade unions were pressing for better education to meet the demands of industry.

● Fears existed that Britain's industrial rivals were becoming better educated.

The 1870 Act

The Act did not replace the existing voluntary school system but aimed to provide schools where there were none. In districts where there were no schools or not enough places, **school boards** were set up. Members were elected by the local ratepayers. These Boards:

● provided elementary schools for 5 to 10-year-olds where none existed;

● built and maintained schools funded by rates and government grants;

● charged fees for attendance.

School attendance was not made compulsory. Religious education in state schools was simple Bible teaching. The Act allowed parents to withdraw their children from scripture lessons.

However, the Act had its opponents:

● The voluntary societies objected to a rival system of state schools.

● Other bodies argued that the voluntary schools should come under state control.

● Religious bodies were concerned about religious teaching in state schools.

The Act set up the first system of state schools and thousands of elementary schools were built. Other acts followed.

KEY IDEAS

Education became more important because of:

● the 1867 Reform Act

● industrial rivalry from abroad

Mundella's Act, 1880
● made attendance compulsory
● set the minimum leaving age at 10
● allowed part-time attendance between the ages of 10 and 13

Free Schooling Act, 1891
● allowed parents the right to demand free elementary education

---

In 1893, the minimum leaving age was raised to 11, and was raised again – to 12 – in 1899.

By 1900 there were about 2,500 school boards in England and Wales running 5,700 schools. However, there was still a need for improvement. The voluntary societies' schools were less well equipped and funded than the board schools. There was still no state-provided secondary education although a small number of school boards illegally provided it.

Questions

1. Why was it thought necessary to 'Educate our masters'?

2. Make a list of the reasons for the passing of the 1870 Education Act.

3. Do you think all these reasons are equally important, or are some more important than the others?

15.5 *Do equal educational opportunities exist* ?

The 1902 Education Act

The need for elementary education for all children had been recognised in the late 19th century. By 1900 it was clear that for Britain to keep up with its commercial rival, Germany, there was also a great need for secondary education. The Education Act of 1902 ('Balfour's Act') abolished school boards. Local education authorities (LEAs), run by the local councils, took over the responsibility of the existing elementary schools. They also had to provide secondary education. However, for children to attend secondary school they had to win scholarships, or their parents had to be able to afford the fees. This meant that many children could not go to secondary school, even though in 1918 the school leaving age was raised to 14. These children remained at elementary school.

The 1944 Education Act

The Second World War drove home the importance of education in a modern industrial society. Post-war educational development was based on the major extension and re-organisation brought about

> ### KEY IDEAS
>
> - Limited access to secondary education from 1902
>
> - Children selected for different kinds of schools at age 11
>
> - Comprehensive education introduced
>
> - Impact of curriculum provision

by the Education Act, 1944 (the 'Butler Act'). The main terms of the Act were:
- Fees were abolished in all state secondary schools.
- The school leaving age was to be raised to 15 as soon as possible. (This happened in 1947, and in 1973 it was raised to 16.)
- LEAs had to provide both primary (ages 5-11) and secondary education (from age 11).
- Children were to receive an education

SOURCE 17
A drawing to show the division made by the 11-plus. Do you think this gives a fair interpretation? ▲

'I'm afraid we don't have much time for teaching here – we're too busy examining.'

SOURCE 18 ▲
The impact of testing.

suited to their 'age, aptitude and ability'. In secondary education this resulted in the creation of secondary grammar, secondary modern, and secondary technical schools.

- Maximum class sizes were to be forty in primary schools and thirty in secondary.
- LEAs had to provide school meals, free milk and regular medical inspections.

It was left to the LEAs to choose how they selected which children should go to the grammar school. Most opted for a test of English, arithmetic and intelligence to be taken in the last year at primary school (see Source 25 page 175). This test became known as the '**11-plus**'. Critics argued that the 11-plus tests were unreliable and put pressure on primary schools. Reports showed that selection at the age of 11 was sometimes unfair and inaccurate. Although in theory, the secondary modern schools were as good as the grammar schools, in practice they came to be regarded as second-rate. Grammar schools tended to take children from middle-class backgrounds.

Comprehensive schools

In the 1960s a growing dissatisfaction with selection methods led many people to support the idea of comprehensive education. Under this system all children in an area went to the same secondary school which catered for every level of ability. In 1965 the development of comprehensive schooling became official Labour Party policy. By the late 1980s, 90% of children were educated in comprehensive schools.

Curriculum and assessment

In 1951 the **General Certificate of Education** (GCE) was introduced. 'O' (ordinary) and 'A' (advanced) level examinations became available for brighter children. In 1965 the **Certificate of Secondary Education** (CSE) was introduced for those below GCE 'O' level ability. In 1986 a new examination course was introduced, the **General Certificate of Secondary Education** (GCSE) replacing GCE and CSE for 16-year-olds.

The Education Act of 1988 introduced the **National Curriculum**. This gives the Government the power to decide what is taught in schools. Programmes of Study were developed for ten subjects, with tests for all children at the ages of 7, 11 and 14 in English, mathematics and science. The same Act allowed schools to 'opt out' of local authority control and become grant-maintained (which means funded directly by the Government). Despite these changes the debate on what sort of education should be provided has continued. The emphasis is now placed on literacy and numeracy in the primary school.

Questions

1. Give two reasons why it was thought necessary to pass the 1944 Education Act.

2. How was education reorganised by this Act?

3. What were the effects of this reorganisation?

Looking back over your study of education:

4. How and why has the curriculum changed during this period?

5. Is the education system more effective now than at any time before?

15.6 *The comprehensive debate*

Increasingly in the late 1940s and early 1950s, the 11-plus examination was criticised. It brought stress and strain to children and their families, and affected the education received in the primary school. The examination was said to be biased in favour of children with middle-class backgrounds. The secondary modern schools had an overwhelming proportion of working-class children, while the grammar schools were mainly filled by middle-class children. Not everyone, however, agreed with comprehensive education. There were fears that it would reduce standards with the brighter children suffering most. One of the main criticisms was the damaging psychological effects on children of attending large schools with up to 2,000 pupils.

SOURCE 19

A historian has noted:

Children stood more chance of passing the 11-plus in some parts of the country than in others. In Wales more than one-third of children were going to grammar schools, but in Surrey only one in seven were selected.

A BIASED SYSTEM

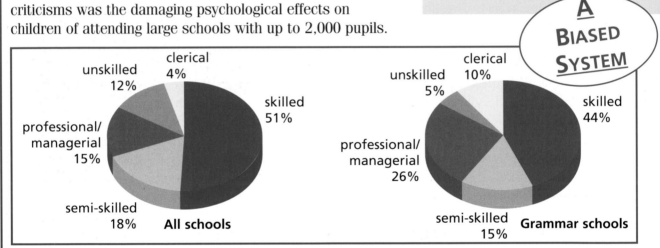

SOURCE 20 ▲
The occupational background of fathers of pupils at secondary school in 1954.

SOURCE 21

This view was expressed in the early 1960s by a group supporting the Labour Party:

To achieve genuine equality of educational opportunity, we need to reorganise the state secondary schools on comprehensive lines.

SOURCE 22

K. Harry Ree, in The Essential Grammar School, *1956, claimed:*

Selection has meant that the clever child has been able to work alongside children equally clever, and has therefore gained from pitting his or her mind against a mind of similar calibre.

EDUCATION SUITED TO ABILITY

SOURCE 23 ▶
A Government report published in 1943 described these aims:

For the academic child there should be the secondary grammar school; for the mechanically minded there should be the technical school; whilst for the essentially practical pupil there should remain the secondary modern school.

MARKED FOR LIFE

The 11-plus examination comes out as a highly reliable and remarkably valid instrument of prediction. Nevertheless errors do happen. Whether a 10 per cent error across the whole country, involving about 60,000 children per year is to be regarded as reasonable or intolerable, largely depends upon what particular values are regarded as most important.

SOURCE 24 ▶
From The Report on Admission to Grammar Schools, *1964.*

◀ **SOURCE 25**
Attendance Card for the 11-plus examination.

> S.S.A.9
> LANCASHIRE EDUCATION COMMITTEE
> Division 9.
>
> Examination for Selection for Secondary Schools
> SATURDAY, 18th FEBRUARY, 1956
> ADMIT Raymond Derek ENNION
> to the Examination at   Room E
> **Turton County Secondary School,**
> Chapeltown Road, Bromley Cross,
> Nr. Bolton.
>
> Name of Centre TURTON
> Candidate's Examination No. 241
>
>   T. B. WILLIS,
> Education Office,   Divisional Education Officer.
> Darwen.
>
> **TIME TABLE OF EXAMINATION**
>
> Time   Subject
> 9-30 a.m. to 10-10 a.m.   Arithmetic
>   Interval
> 10-40 a.m. to 11-20 a.m.   English
>   Interval
> 11-35 a.m. to 12-15 p.m.   Intelligence Test.
>
> The Candidate must bring this Admission Card to the Examination Centre
>   P.T.O.

SOURCE 26 ▶
A child carrying a placard at an anti-selection protest in 1970.

Hospital beds for 11-plus

FROM OUR CORRESPONDENT
BIRMINGHAM, OCT. 29
Almost a third of the young patients being treated by a consultant psychiatrist at Birmingham Children's Hospital are suffering from emotional stress caused by worry over ...

The headmaster of an independent school said a possible cause of the trouble was the tendency of some parents to get "panic-stricken" as the examination approached.

Equal to it

◀ **SOURCE 27**
This headline is from the front page of The Times, *30 October 1967. The article describes how children needed psychiatric help because of the stress of the 11-plus exam.*

Questions

1. According to Source 23, what schools were available for a child aged over 11 to attend in the period immediately following the 1944 Education Act.

2. How useful are Sources 24 and 25 in explaining how reliable 11-plus selection was?

3. According to Sources 21 and 23 what are the benefits of selection at age 11?

4. Do Sources 19 and 20 support the view expressed in Source 22?

5. Does Source 27 fully explain the actions of the child shown in Source 26? Use your own knowledge to help answer the question.

6. Do all these sources adequately represent the arguments for and against selection at age 11?

16 THE CHANGING ROLE & STATUS OF WOMEN

16.1 *What was the role and status of women in mid-Victorian society*?

What was women's position in the early 19th century?

In the early 19th century there were few opportunities for girls and women. Usually they lived under male dominance. They first had to obey their father and then, if they married, their husband.

Girls had limited educational opportunities. If girls from working-class families had any education at all it was very basic. Most girls from better-off families just learned social graces including, singing, painting and playing the piano.

Women could not follow professions such as medicine. Those from better-off families, who needed to earn a living, could be governesses. For working-class women, domestic service was the most common paid employment. Servants often worked long hours at hard and dirty jobs. Women also worked in factories and coal-mines. Pay was poor for all these jobs.

Women had few political rights. They could not vote in Parliamentary elections. They could not be Members of Parliament or of the House of Lords. Even Queen Victoria called the movement for women's rights a *'mad, wicked folly'*.

Florence Nightingale commented in 1851 that *'Women don't*

consider themselves as human beings at all, there is absolutely no God, no country, no duty to them at all except family'. A woman's main role was to marry, have children, bring them up, and provide a comfortable home for her husband. Cooking, cleaning and washing were tiring, lengthy jobs. As there was no cheap contraception available, many women had one pregnancy after another while they went on doing heavy **household work**.

Anything a married woman had, or earned, legally belonged to her husband. It was up to her husband to decide how much housekeeping money she had to feed and clothe the family.

SOURCE 1 ▲
A 'sweated workshop'.

Beginnings of change

During the 19th century, employment began to be separated into 'men's work' which was better paid and 'women's work'.

In the middle of the 18th century there had been as many male as female servants. By the middle of the 19th century most servants were women. **Domestic service** became seen as 'women's work'.

Lord Shaftesbury was appalled at the harsh conditions suffered by women working in factories and mines. He also did not like women working outside the home. The result of his campaign for change was a series of laws limiting the work that women could do:

- **Mines Act, 1842** prevented women from working underground.
- **Factory Act, 1844** limited a woman's working day to 12 hours.
- **Ten Hours Act, 1847** limited women to 10 hours per day in textile factories.
- **Factory Act, 1867** limited women to 10 hours a day in any work place employing more than 50 people.

These laws protected women from bad working conditions but also limited their earnings. When their working hours were cut women could no longer work in factories as men's equals and their wages fell. Women were pushed into lower-paid work such as the **'sweated trades'** (see Source 1). They worked at home or in small workshops sewing, making candles or match boxes. Many women turned to prostitution.

SOURCE 2

Hannah Cullwick, a domestic servant, kept a diary. This is what she wrote for 14 July 1860:

I opened the shutters and lit the kitchen fire. Swept and dusted the rooms and the hall. Laid the breakfast table and got breakfast. Made the beds and emptied the slops, cleared and washed the breakfast things up. Cleaned the silver and cleaned the knives. Got dinner ready. Cleaned the steps and the floor on my knees, polished the boot scraper at the front of the house and cleaned the pavement outside the house on my knees. Cleaned the pantry, scoured the table, scrubbed the flags around the house. Made tea for the master at nine. Cleaned the privy and scullery floor. Put supper ready.

16.2 *How far did attitudes towards women change by 1900*?

Improvements in women's legal position

Several Acts of Parliament in the second half of the 19th century improved women's lives. Women successfully campaigned for the right to own property. The **Married Women's Property Act, 1870**, gave married women the right to own property and to keep their earnings. This right was strengthened by another Act in 1882.

Women also campaigned to be able to get a divorce on the same grounds as men. The **Matrimonial Clauses Act, 1857**, introduced a simpler and cheaper system of divorce. Women could bring divorce cases against their husbands for cruelty, desertion and adultery. However, the Act made it easier for men to divorce their wives for adultery alone, while women also had to prove that their husbands had either been cruel or deserted them.

In 1886 the **Married Woman's Act** meant a husband who deserted his wife had to pay maintenance. Also in 1886, the **Guardianship of Infants Act** allowed widowed mothers to become the legal guardian of their children. From 1891 women could not be forced to stay in their husbands' homes against their will.

New job opportunities

Careers began to open up for women. Following Florence Nightingale's work in the Crimean War, schools for the training of nurses were set up. Nursing became a popular career for women. Elizabeth Garrett Anderson started as a nurse at the Middlesex Hospital and, despite much hostility, became the first woman doctor to practice in England. In 1876 an Act of Parliament allowed medical schools to admit women students.

The number of schools increased, particularly after the 1870 Education Act, so more teachers were needed. By 1900, three-quarters of teachers were women. However, if a woman teacher got married she had to resign.

> ## KEY IDEAS
> - Women's legal position improved
> - New job opportunities developed
> - Education was more readily available

SOURCE 3
The Post Office was a major employer of women in new jobs, such as operating the new switchboards. ▼

As commerce developed there was more office work. The invention of the typewriter and telephone also provided work opportunities (Source 3). Gradually male clerks were replaced by less well-paid women clerks.

Nursing, teaching and office work appealed to middle-class women, but new opportunities also opened up for working-class women. The growth of shops and department stores increased demand for shop assistants. Hours were often long, sometimes up to 80 hours per week. However, this was less than in domestic service, and shop girls had evenings and Sundays free.

Education

Demand for equality in education for women increased. In 1848 Queen's College, London

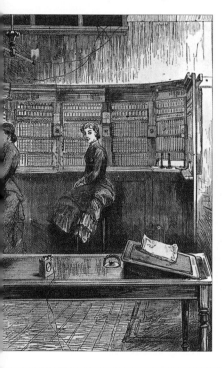

was founded for training women teachers. From the 1850s ladies colleges were set up, such as the North London Collegiate School founded by Frances Mary Buss. These provided a good all-round education for girls of a standard equal to the best boys' schools. Wealthy

middle-class families began sending their daughters to boarding school. Many of these were modelled on the Cheltenham College for Young Ladies founded by Dorothea Beale in 1858.

A university education was the passport to the best jobs and careers such as medicine and the law. To compete with men, women needed to go to university. In 1873, Girton College, Cambridge, was founded for women, but Cambridge University would not allow women to take degrees. However, in 1878, London University allowed women to take degrees on the same terms as men.

Although things were changing, the attitude of society towards women would take many more years to alter.

SOURCE 5

Caroline Norton had a very unhappy marriage. She left her husband and found that she could not get a divorce – she lost the right to see her children. Her husband tried to take all the money she earned from writing novels. In 1855 she wrote to Queen Victoria:

A married woman has no legal existence of her own. Years of separation cannot alter this position. Her property is his property. Her husband may take it and sell as he pleases even though they may be gifts from relatives and friends or bought before marriage. A wife cannot legally claim her own earnings. Her salary is the husband's.

SOURCE 4

A school inspector writing in 1874 thought:

A girl is not necessarily a better woman because she knows the heights of all the mountains in Europe, and can work a fraction in her head; but she is decidedly better fitted for the duties she will be called upon to perform if she knows how to wash and tend a child, cook simple food well and thoroughly clean a house.

Questions

1. Describe the jobs available to working-class women in the first half of the 19th century. (See pages 176-177.)

2. What effect did changes in the law have on the availability of work for women?

3. How different were the types of jobs becoming available towards the end of the 19th century?

4. How far was the legal position of women, like Caroline Norton (Source 5), improved in the 19th century?

16.3 Why had women not been given the vote by 1914?

The political position of women in 1900

The second half of the 19th century saw some progress in women's political rights. Following the 1870 Education Act, women were allowed to vote in elections for school boards, and to sit on the new boards. After 1888 women ratepayers were allowed to vote in county council and county borough elections. The Reform Acts of 1867 and 1884 had given the vote to the majority of men, but not to women. The main issue became women's right to vote for, and sit as, Members of Parliament.

Some people argued that it was 'unfeminine' for women to get mixed up in politics. Some thought that women would not be able to judge political issues sensibly.

DYING FOR THE CAUSE

SOURCE 6
On 5 June 1913, The Times *reported Emily Davison's death:* ▼

The Derby of 1913 will long remain memorable. The desperate act of the woman who rushed from the rails on to the course, as the horses swept round Tattenham Corner, apparently from some mad notion that she could spoil the race, will impress the general public. She did not interfere with the race, but she nearly killed a jockey as well as herself, and she brought down a valuable horse. A deed of this kind, we need hardly say, is not likely to increase the popularity of the cause with the public. Persons who wantonly destroy property and endanger lives must be either desperately wicked, or entirely unbalanced.

SOURCE 7
The Times *also reported a different view of the event:* ▼

Some of the spectators close to the woman said that she seemed to think that the horses had all gone by and that she was just trying to cross the course.

UNFIT FOR POWER

SOURCE 8
An MP commented after Emily Davison's death, 5 June 1913: ▼

People who thoughtlessly destroy property and put lives in danger must be either wicked or totally unbalanced.

SOURCE 9
An MP speaking against giving women the vote said: ▼

The government of the country would be handed over to a majority who would not be men, but women. Women are creatures of impulses and emotion and do not decide questions on the ground of reason as men do. What does one find when one gets into the company of women and talks politics? One is soon asked to stop talking silly politics, and yet this is the type to whom we are invited to hand over the destinies of the country. It is not only that women are unfitted by their physical nature to exercise political power, but also that the majority of them do not want it.

SOURCE 10
The Derby, 4 June 1913. Emily Davison is on the left. She has not yet hit the ground. ▼

The 'suffragists'

In 1897 the **National Union of Women's Suffrage Societies** (NUWSS) was formed by Mrs Millicent Fawcett. Known as the 'suffragists', they believed in a **policy of persuasion** – hoping through meetings, petitions, reasoned argument, legal propaganda and the threat of tax avoidance, to persuade Parliament to grant their demands.

The 'suffragettes'

Some women thought that the progress being made by the suffragists was too slow, and so the **Women's Social and Political Union** (WSPU), led by Emmeline Pankhurst and her daughter Christabel, was founded in Manchester in 1903. They were soon joined by Emmeline's daughter Sylvia.

The 'suffragettes' aimed to attract publicity for their cause and to annoy the Government as much as possible. They were prepared to be more violent than their rival the National Union, and are often called '**militant**'.

The Government and the courts took firm action. When the suffragettes were arrested they were fined by the courts. When they refused to pay they were sent to prison. In prison, many suffragettes went on hunger strike. They had to be forcibly fed – which was painful and dangerous. This aroused a public outcry about force-feeding.

To defeat the hunger strikers, in 1913 the Government introduced the '**Cat and Mouse**' **Act**. This allowed a hunger striker to be released, then re-arrested when she had recovered. Opponents claimed that the Act was like a cat playing cruelly with a mouse. Because of the Act, Emmeline Pankhurst went in and out of prison twelve times in 1913.

Suffragette tactics included:

- **heckling** members of the Government at public meetings. This was done to Winston Churchill in Manchester in 1905. Christabel Pankhurst and Annie Kenny were thrown out of the meeting;
- **chaining** themselves to the railings of Buckingham Palace;
- **assaulting politicians** who were known to oppose votes for women;
- **making attacks on public property**, slashing pictures in the National Gallery and breaking shop windows;
- **arson attacks**. Pillar boxes were set on fire and even houses and churches.

The most famous single incident happened in 1913 when **Emily Davison**, a leading suffragette, drew attention to the women's cause by throwing herself in front of King George V's horse in the Derby at Epsom. She was killed.

Moderate suffragette leaders became increasingly concerned about the rise in violence. Many thought that the campaign was out of control. Violence played into the hands of those against extending suffrage to women such as the Prime Minister, Asquith. He argued that giving in to threats would encourage others, such as the dockers and miners, to try similar methods. The use of violence also turned many moderate MPs against the movement, including some who had previously shown support.

FORCE FEEDING

SOURCE 12

Mary Leigh, a prominent suffragette described force feeding:

> The sensation is most painful. The drums of the ears seem to be bursting and there is a horrible pain in the throat and breast. I have to lie on the bed, pinned down by two wardresses, one doctor stands on a chair holding the funnel end at arm's length, and the other doctor forces the other end up the nostrils. The one holding the funnel end pours the liquid down.

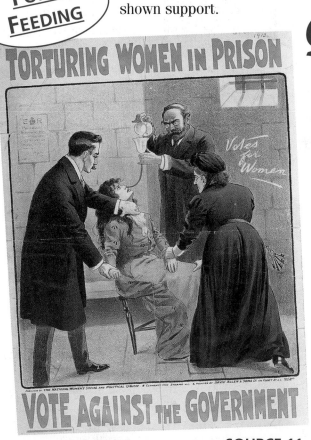

▲ **SOURCE 11**
An election poster. Probably for the 1910 election.

Questions

1. What does Source 10 tell you about the events at the 1913 Derby?

2. Does Source 6 support this view?

3. Source 10 is a photograph and Source 6 is from a newspaper. Does this mean they are both useful to a historian studying the events of 4 June 1913?

4. Look at Sources 6, 7 and 8. These sources give different views of the events. Explain why there are these differences.

5. Read Source 9. Why did attitudes like this exist at the time?

6. What were the motives behind the issue of the election poster (Source 11)?

7. Are you able to use the information on pages 180-182 to explain fully why women had not been given the vote by 1914? Explain your answer.

16.4 How did the First World War help women gain the vote?

On the outbreak of the First World War in 1914, the suffragettes abandoned their campaign of violence and pledged full support to the war effort. During the war, women filled many of the jobs that had belonged to men who had gone away to fight. Women worked as drivers and conductors on trains and buses, and they made weapons in munitions factories. Women also joined women's branches of the armed forces, and served as nurses with the army and in military hospitals.

During the war, the Government realised it had a problem. The voting system required voters to live in the same place for twelve months before an election. So, if an election was called, most soldiers would not be able to vote. The Government decided to change the law. Women's groups saw their opportunity. They put pressure on the Government to include votes for women in the changes. The Government also hoped that if it gave women the vote they would be grateful and vote for the Government.

In 1918 Parliament passed new laws which gave all women over 30 the vote and the right to sit as MPs. Before the war many men had feared that women would take over Parliament. However, in 1918 only seventeen women stood as candidates, and Lady Astor became the first woman to sit in the House of Commons.

> **KEY IDEAS**
> - The war changed attitudes to women
> - The franchise was expanded after the war

SOURCE 13 ▲
Women working in a munitions factory during the First World War.

SOURCE 14

Asquith, the Prime Minister, speaking in August 1916 said:

It is true that women cannot fight in the sense of going out with rifles, but they have aided in the most effective way. What is more, when the war comes to an end, have not the women a special claim to be heard on the many questions which will arise affecting their interests? I cannot deny that claim.

Questions

1. What does Source 13 tell you about women's work during the First World War?

2. Look at Source 14. How important in achieving the vote was the work undertaken by women during the War?

16.5 How far did the position of women change in the inter-war period?

Campaigners for women's rights expected that the granting of the vote would also bring about wider social changes, and improvements in the position and status of women.

Changes in politics

In 1928 the **Equal Franchise Act** gave all women over the age of 21 the right to vote. This had been one of the main aims of both the suffragists and the suffragettes. Women could now vote on the same terms as men. They formed just over 50% of the electorate, and yet only 67 women stood as candidates in the 1931 general election. Men still dominated Parliament and political life.

SOURCE 15

Mrs Millicent Fawcett, the campaigner for Women's rights, wrote in 1928:

It is almost exactly 61 years ago since I heard John Stuart Mill introduce his suffrage amendment to the Reform Bill on May 20th, 1867. So I have had extraordinary good luck in having seen the struggle from the beginning.

KEY IDEAS

- Women achieved equal voting rights to men
- Legal position improved
- Birth control became more common

Impact on work

At the end of the First World War women were expected to return to looking after the home and family, or to traditional 'women's work' such as domestic service or dressmaking. Women who tried to hold on to their war-time jobs were criticised by men.

Most women did not want to return to the poorly-paid jobs of the pre-war period – their new jobs had given them more money, greater freedom and improved status. But they had no choice. Women's wages were often only half of those of men, so trade unions feared that women were a threat to men's jobs. As women often did not belong to trade unions they were unable to bargain for improved working conditions and pay.

SOURCE 16

Changes in rights and position of women, 1918-1930. ▼

1918 Women over 30 get vote. First woman MP elected.

1919 Sex Disqualification Removal Act. Women can not longer be barred from a job because of their sex. Only applies to single women.

SOURCE 17
Amy Johnson. ▼

As a result of the **Sex Disqualification Removal Act** in 1919, women were able to hold public office, enter universities, and become lawyers and magistrates. In 1925, women were allowed to work in the Civil Service for the first time. The Sex Disqualification Removal Act, however, had little effect on the career prospects of most women. Equal pay was not the reward for equal work. The Act also only applied to single women. A woman could still lose her job if she married.

In the later 1920s and the 1930s, new industries grew up which brought new jobs. Women were happy to take jobs assembling radios and telephones. Banking and office-work continued to grow, increasing the availability of jobs for women. But this was not universal over the country as in the depressed areas there were not enough jobs for men.

Other changes

In 1923 women were granted equal rights to men in divorce cases.

The use of birth control inside marriage became more acceptable and Marie Stopes opened a clinic in London in 1921. In 1930 the Government agreed to make **contraceptive advice** available to women and started the National Birth-Control Council. In 1939 it changed its name to the Family Planning Association. This gave women the choice of having children or not.

Greater freedom developed with younger women wearing clothing that was much simpler and less restrictive. Make-up became acceptable, and women went to the cinema and dances with boyfriends and without a chaperone. The First World War had given women greater confidence and they were becoming more and more successful. An example of this success was Amy Johnson, who in 1930, became the first woman to fly solo to Australia. Women like Amy Johnson became role models.

In 1937 the *Daily Telegraph* commented *'How the Historian of 100 years ago would be confounded if he could return and see the woman of today. He would find women engineers, architects, lawyers, accountants, doctors, dentists, vets, librarians, journalists, scientists, tax inspectors and factory inspectors'.*

Questions

1. Using the timeline (Source 16), describe the changes to the role and status of women in the period 1918-1939.

2. Look at Source 15. Why did it take so long for women to gain the vote?

3. How important were people like Amy Johnson in changing the way women were viewed?

1923 Women given equal rights to men in divorce cases.

1925 Women allowed to join civil service. Women given same rights over their children as men.

1928 Equal Franchise Act gives all women over the age of 21 the right to vote.

1929 Margaret Bondfield becomes first woman Cabinet Minister.

1930 Government makes contraceptive advice available to women.

16.6 Has the battle for women's rights been won?

The Second World War

During the Second World War (1939-1945) women were expected to work in industry, on farms, as nurses and in the armed forces. They carried out many of the roles and duties as they had done during the First World War. There were, however, some important differences to the effect of the war on women's lives.

SOURCE 18

A representative of the Law Society made these comments on BBC Radio, April 1995:

Fifty per cent of people entering the profession are women. Twenty-five to thirty per cent of people practising as solicitors are women. Yet in a big city law firm, with hundreds of partners, only half a dozen will be women. Women tend to get pushed into doing matrimonial work while men take other work. Women are assumed just to be doing the job to fill their time before they go off to have a family.

SOURCE 19 ▲
In recent years men have increasingly taken on what traditionally have been women's roles.

- Bombing raids on the towns and cities of Britain, strict food rationing, and the evacuation of children greatly affected the lives of women in Britain.
- From 1941 every woman had to register for war work.
- There was less resistance from the unions about women taking men's jobs. Even so, after the end of the war married women had to give up their jobs.

Equal opportunities?

The first effective contraceptive pill became available in the 1960s. This allowed increased opportunities for women to plan having children to fit in with their careers. 'The Pill' gave women greater freedom and equality.

Many more women attended university from the 1960s. With equal educational prospects, many women were becoming frustrated that the best jobs were still closed to them. This resulted in the growth of the 'women's liberation movement' which in the longer term gave women confidence to assert their rights. The movement found it was difficult to change attitudes and it was not popular with everyone. It was seen by some as a threat to a stable family life.

you set it... and forget it!

BENDIX

automatically gives you . . . the time of your life!

SOURCE 20 ▲
Washing machine advertisement.

◀ **SOURCE 21**
Anita Roddick, a successful business woman.

The **Equal Pay Act** of 1970 stated that employers should pay women the same wage as men if they were doing a similar job. This Act came into effect in 1975. The **Sex Discrimination Act** 1975 made discrimination on the grounds of sex illegal. This affected jobs, housing and other areas. The **Equal Opportunities Commission** was also set up by the Act to examine allegations of discrimination against women.

The increasing use of electricity and a revolution in the availability of labour-saving devices for the home have helped to liberate married as well as single women. These modern gadgets, changes in the way food is prepared and smaller families have enabled women to both go out to work and run a home.

Equal or not?

It has been difficult for women to enter the professions. In 1980 only 8% of barristers and 1% of accountants were women. In 1983 only 23 out of 650 MPs were women. Margaret Thatcher became Britain's first woman Prime Minister in 1979, but until the 1997 election there have been few female cabinet ministers.

Women still tend to do the lower paid jobs. In 1975, 92% of nurses and 81% of shop assistants were women. Average earnings of women are still less than those of men. Women have made great advances in education, and girls do better than boys at school, yet fewer girls go on to further and higher education. In more recent times some men have chosen to take the main responsibility for bringing up their children while their wives or partners continue to work (Source 19).

Images of women

Since the 1960s, some women have campaigned against discrimination by men. These people are known as feminists. They said it was unjust to force women to be anything they did not want to be. Some objected to little girls playing with baby dolls because it encouraged them to think of traditional female roles in the home. They protested about pin-ups of women because they saw it as a way in which men used women. Some of their complaints did make people change their attitudes. For example, female rape victims are treated with much more sympathy than before. Other complaints got nowhere. Some feminists objected to Miss World and other beauty competitions, but these still exist.

In the 1990s many people have attempted to show images of women as ordinary people, living ordinary lives, but

SOURCE 22

The Low Pay Unit in 1995 noted:

According to the *New Earnings Survey 1995*, there are ninety-one occupations which pay below the Council of Europe's decency threshold currently £228.54 a week. From the ninety-one, twenty-four male occupations and seventy-eight female occupations appear below it.

SOURCE 23
The first person under 21 to vote in a British Parliamentary election (1970).

some still argue that women are represented in stereotyped images which ordinary women try to – but cannot – live up to. An example of this is when wafer-thin models are portrayed as the ideal woman.

In 1997 the pop group the Spice Girls developed the idea of 'Girl Power'. This resulted in certain advertisements which attracted complaints from men who found them demeaning (Source 25).

It seems as if the roles of both women and men in society are still changing.

SOURCE 25

An article in the Express *12 November 1997 described the phenomena of 'Girl Power':*

Girl Power, as defined by the Spice Girls, is proving to be way over the top for men. They are said to find it demeaning, and companies were warned yesterday to go easy on the current trend for adverts showing violent images of women in control. The Advertising Standards Authority say some posters are attracting a growing number of complaints. Opponents of the trend say Girl Power is simply violence dressed up as equality.

Questions

1. Describe the attempts made by Government since 1945 to change the role and status of women.

2. How have changes in the following affected the position of women in the 20th century:
   (a) education;
   (b) household labour-saving machines;
   (c) contraception?

3. Margaret Thatcher, on becoming Prime Minister' in 1979, said 'The Battle for women's rights has largely been won.' Do you agree?

INDEX

Acknowledgments

Every effort has been made to contact the holders of copyright material, but if any have been inadvertently overlooked the publishers will be pleased to make the necessary arrangements at the first opportunity.

The publishers would like to thank the following for permission to reproduce photographs (T=Top, B=Bottom, C=Centre, L=Left, R=Right):

Cover photos. T, Terry Gorman/Mastercraft Fine Arts; C, Statens Museum für Kunst, Copenhagen/Bridgeman Art Library; B, Bonhams, London/Bridgeman Art Library.

Mary Evans Picture Library, p 4; Getty Images, p 5; Fotomas Index, p 7; Fine Art Society; London/Bridgeman Art Library, London & New York, pp 8/9; Rural History Centre, University of Reading, p 9; Rural History Centre, University of Reading, pp 12 & 13; Fotomas Index, p 15; Bedfordshire & Luton Archives Office, p 16; Fotomas Index, p 19; Fotomas Index, p 22; Getty Images, p 22; Rural History Centre, University of Reading, p 24BL; Getty Images, p 24T; Rural History Centre, University of Reading, p 25; Fotomas Index, p 26; Rural History Centre, University of Reading, p 27; ILN Picture Library, pp 28/29; Mary Evans Picture Library, p 30; Fotomas Index, p 31; Getty Images, p 32; IACR-Rothamsted, p 34; Getty Images, p 35; Mary Evans Picture Library, p 37; Mary Evans Picture Library, pp 38/39; Fotomas Index, p 39R; Arkwright Society, p 40 & 41T; Mary Evans Picture Library p 41B; Fotomas Index, p 43; Colne Local Studies Library, Lancashire pp 44/45; Fotomas Index, p 46L; Leeds Library & Information Services, pp 46/47; Ironbridge Gorge Museum Trust, p 51; Fotomas Index, pp 52/53; Fotomas Index, p 54T; Science Museum/Science & Society Picture Library, p 54B; Mary Evans Picture Library, p 59; Mary Evans Picture Library, p 61; Fotomas Index, pp 62/63; Fotomas Index, pp 64 & 65; Fotomas Index p 67; Mary Evans Picture Library, pp 68 & 70; Fotomas Index, pp 71 & 73; Getty Images, pp 74/75 & 75R; Getty Images, p 76; Fotomas Index, p 77; Ray Ennion, p 78; Getty Images, p 79; Mary Evans Picture Library, p 80; Getty Images, p 81;

Ray Ennion, p 82L; Getty Images, p 82T; Getty Images, p 83; Fotomas Index, pp 84/85; Getty Images, p 87; Ironbridge Gorge Museum Trust, p 89T; Getty Images, p 89B; British Waterways Archive, Gloucester, p 92; Fotomas Index, p 93; Fotomas Index, pp 94 & 95; Liverpool Record Office, Liverpool Libraries & Information Services, p 96T; Getty Images, p 96CL & R; Fotomas Index, p 97; Mary Evans Picture Library, p 98; ILN Picture Library, p 102; Mary Evans Picture Library, p 103; Getty Images, pp 104/5; Punch Cartoon Library, pp 106 & 107; Wellcome Institute, p 108; Punch Cartoon Library, p 110; Mary Evans Picture Library, p 111; Maurice Harvey/Polytint Cards, p 112; Fotomas Index, p 114; Getty Images, p 116; Science Museum/Science & Society Picture Library, p 118; Science Photo Library, p 122; Rex Features Ltd, p 123; Stafford Local Studies Library, p 124; Getty Images, p 129; Getty Images, p 131T; Mary Evans Picture Library, p 131B; E.T. Archive, p 134; Barnardos, p 135T; Mary Evans Picture Library, p 135B; E.T. Archive, pp 136/7; Getty Images, p 141; Fotomas Index, pp 144/5; Fotomas Index, pp 146/7; Fotomas Index, p 148; Mary Evans Picture Library, p 150; ILN Picture Library, p 152, Popperfoto, p 153; Rail; Maritime & Transport Union, p 154; PA' News Photo Library, p 156T; Getty Images, p 156B; Robert Opie Collection, p 157; PA; News Photo Library, p 159; T. Kirk/ Camera Press; p 161; Fotomas Index, pp 162/3; Fotomas Index, pp 164/5; Mary Evans Picture Library, p 166; Ray Ennion, p 167, Punch Cartoon Library, p 170; ILN Picture Library, pp 176/7; Getty Images, pp 178/9; Getty Images, pp 180/1; Fotomas Index, p 182; Imperial War Museum; London p 183; Getty Images, p 185; Judy Harrison/Format Photographers, p 186; Robert Opie Collection, p 187T; PA' News Photo Library, pp 187B & 188; Brenda Prince/Format Photographers, p 189.

The publishers are grateful to the following for permission to reproduce previously published material: Harrap, for an extract from P. Gregg, *A Social and Economic History of Britain 1760-1815*, 1982; Heinemann for an extract from Robert Hulme, *Education Since 1700*, 1989; Wayland Publishers Ltd for an extract from Howard Hughes, *Alexander Fleming and Penicillin*, 1974,